ISLAMIC AFRICA

ISLAMIC AFRICA

Formerly SUDANIC AFRICA

ISLAMIC AFRICA

VOLUME 1, ISSUE 1 SPRING 2010

Northwestern University Press
Evanston, Illinois

www.islamicafricajournal.org

Scope and Mission: *Islamic Africa* is a peer-reviewed, multidisciplinary, academic journal published by Northwestern University Press in collaboration with the Institute for the Study of Islamic Thought in Africa (ISITA), based at Northwestern University, Evanston, Illinois. The journal incorporates *Sudanic Africa,* retaining its focus on historical sources, bibliographies, and methodologies. *Islamic Africa* promotes interaction between scholars of Islam and Africa across all continents and across historical periods. The journal welcomes papers from the humanities and the social sciences on any aspect of Islam and Muslim life pertaining to Africa, or originating from the African continent.

Communications concerning manuscripts and editorial matters should be addressed to Prof. M. Sani Umar, Editor, *Islamic Africa,* Northwestern University Press, 629 Noyes Street, Evanston, IL 60208 (USA); islamicafrica@northwestern.edu. For information about submitting manuscripts, see www.islamicafricajournal.org.

Concerning advertising and subscriptions, address the Managing Editor, Gianna F. Mosser, Northwestern University Press, 629 Noyes Street, Evanston, IL 60208 (USA); islamicafrica@northwestern.edu. Electronic subscriptions can be purchased for institutions ($125) and individuals ($75) by visiting www.islamicafricajournal.org.

Northwestern University Press acknowledges Marianne Jankowski for the interior design and Ahmad Faris for the journal logo. The copy editor for this issue was Christine Molinari.

Islamic Africa
Volume 1, Issue 1
Spring 2010

BOOK REVIEWS

LETTER OF INTRODUCTION FROM THE EDITORIAL COLLECTIVE

M. Sani Umar

I am delighted to introduce the first issue of *Islamic Africa* to the scholars of Islam in Africa and to the broader academic community. To avoid any doubt, *Islamic Africa* is an academic journal devoted to the publication of scholarly materials, not religious propaganda. As its mission statement proclaims, this journal is old and new at the same time, for it continues the excellent traditions of its precursor and builds on those traditions in new and exciting directions. The founding editors envisaged *Islamic Africa* as the premier academic journal in its field. To achieve this ambition, the journal is organized as a collegial endeavor not dependent on any one particular person, but on the collective efforts of individuals willing to serve on thc cditorial board and in other capacities as well as on the continuing interests of the many and diverse readers it hopes to serve. It is being published by a major university press in order to reach as wide a readership as possible and electronically in order to be accessible to audiences beyond the big university libraries. As an electronic journal, *Islamic Africa* hopes to reach more readers than those traditionally served by university libraries in Western Europe and North America.

The intellectual origins of the journal stem from the Institute for the Study of Islamic Thought in Africa (ISITA), established in 2000 by Professor John O. Hunwick of Northwestern University and Professor R. Seán O'Fahey of the University of Bergen. Institutionally located at the Program of African Studies of Northwestern University, ISITA has produced several publications on various aspects of Islam in Africa, hosted visiting

Islamic Africa, VOL. 1, NO. 1, 2010. ISSN 2154-0993. www.islamicafricajournal.org

scholars from Africa and beyond, and organized several conferences at Northwestern University as well as at African academic institutions, creating in the process an international network of intellectual excellence connecting scholars of Islam in Africa in many parts of the world. ISITA was initially conceived to dispel the erroneous but widespread notion that the practice of Islam in Africa south of the Sahara has been devoid of intellectual dimensions—an idea originating largely from the colonially sponsored studies of "Islam Noir/African Islam." Apart from producing impressive scholarship that demonstrates the richness of the Islamic intellectual traditions of Africa, ISITA's research endeavors have also highlighted the many complex connections between Africa and the wider world of Islam. Similarly, the initial ISITA focus on the Islamic intellectual traditions of Africa has since expanded to elucidate the cultural, religious, literary, historical, social, political, and other dimensions within which the now well-documented Islamic intellectual traditions of Africa have been embedded. The exciting scholarship produced under ISITA auspices has been published in major reference works, edited volumes, working papers, and thematic issues of journals. Among the journals, *Sudanic Africa* has been more organically linked with ISITA's intellectual and institutional growth, and *Islamic Africa* incorporates and builds upon this relationship. These organic links will continue to grow and flourish because of the vital elements connecting the two journals, most notably the kind willingness of both the main editor of *Sudanic Africa,* Professor Knut Vikør, and the book review editor, Professor Scott Reese, to serve on the editorial board of *Islamic Africa.*

The intellectual vision of *Islamic Africa* seeks to expand the longstanding traditions of outstanding research and publication about Islam in Africa. To realize this vision, *Islamic Africa* takes advantage of its institutional relationship with Northwestern University, with its formidable assets and unique strengths within its globally famous Program of African Studies, as evidenced, for example, in the award-winning careers of renowned scholars of Islam in Africa, who have also trained dozens of doctoral students in the field. Apart from Northwestern's unmatched library on Africa in general and on Islam in Africa in particular, Northwestern University Press, which has published thirteen volumes in its series on *Islam and Society in Africa*, plans for permanent publication of the journal beyond the initial period of generous seed-funding provided by the Mellon Foundation. Given this excellent intellectual pedigree and prestigious institutional heritage, *Islamic Africa* is poised to extend the frontiers of knowledge in the vibrant and growing field of Islam in Africa broadly understood. Equally significant, this journal seeks to enrich its intellectual reputation by publishing excellent scholarship from the leading specialists and also from the anticipated patronage of readers from broader academic and intellectual communities.

This maiden issue highlights some types of material that *Islamic Africa* will be publishing in the coming years. Thus, in the section continuing with the traditions of *Sudanic Africa,* three authors provide insightful comments on important source documents, bringing deep knowledge to probe the broader intellectual significance of even a fragment of a text, or the preparatory materials and field notes that never made it into print. *Islamic Africa* welcomes submission of source texts analyzed so as to illuminate esoteric aspects that ordinarily would not catch the attention of nonspecialists. In the main section comprising the substantive articles, this issue carries essays that give a very good idea of the multidisciplinary intellectual pursuits that the journal will promote. Richly detailed historical research and meticulous ethnographic work are very much welcome; so also are critical textual studies and discourse analysis—to mention a few. Traditional book reviews of a single volume or more extended commentary on several books on related topics will be published regularly. Other scholarly communications that may grace the pages of this journal include: short notices of research projects, reviews on major conferences, work-in-progress, tributes to departed scholars, and more.

Islamic Africa looks forward to receiving your submissions.

THE NACHTIGAL PAPERS OF THE STAATSBIBLIOTHEK ZU BERLIN

Jörg Adelberger

During a short stay in Berlin at the beginning of 2008, I used the opportunity to have a look at the papers of the explorer Gustav Nachtigal, an undertaking I had in mind since writing my thesis on the Fur of Darfur.[1] My main interest was to gain an impression of the material relating to Darfur.

The major part of the literary estate of Gustav Nachtigal (1834–85) is stored at the Staatsbibliothek Berlin at the Handschriftenabteilung (manuscript department), in the building on Potsdamer Strasse. There are other collections, consisting mainly of letters, at the archive of Justus Perthes Verlag Gotha and at the archive of Leibniz-Institut für Länderkunde at Leipzig.[2]

The Nachtigal Papers at Staatsbibliothek Berlin are organized in two batches. For each batch there is a separate finding aid consisting of inventory lists in a folder. The first batch is made up of several boxes, while the second batch seems to contain only one box, consisting of letters and correspondence. This is from the Sammlung Darmstädter, a collection which was added to the initial estate at a later time.[3]

---

[1] Jörg Adelberger, *Vom Sultanat zur Republik: Veränderungen in der Sozialorganisation der Fur (Sudan)* (Stuttgart: Franz Steiner, 1990).

[2] See http://www.nachlassdatenbank.de/viewall.php?category=N for an overview of the literary estates of Gustav Nachtigal in the German archives.

[3] The Sammlung Darmstädter is a collection that was brought together by Ludwig Darmstädter. In 1907 Darmstädter assigned a huge collection of autographs, consisting of about 6,000 documents, to the Staatsbibliothek.

Islamic Africa, VOL. 1, NO. 1, 2010. ISSN 2154-0993. www.islamicafricajournal.org

In the folder for the first batch there are two lists: one handwritten, one typed. The typed one is essentially a later version of the handwritten one, but the latter contains more details on some items; thus, a researcher should consult both.

Within each box there are several files, and the numbering of these files is significant for retrieval from the storeroom.

One may not order more than two boxes at a time.

The content of the boxes and files is described in fair detail in the inventories, giving the researcher an idea of what he or she may expect.

In conjunction with my fields of interest, I found the following items listed in the finding aid:

Gustav Nachtigal, Batch 1
Box 1:
  File 24—Diaries of journey from Wadai to Darfur, original journal of the journey in Darfur,
  File 25—Description of Darfur
  File 26—Darfur, script of the third volume [of *Sahara und Sudan*][4]
Box 2:
  File 28—Maps; among others, those pertaining to Darfur, Dar Abu Dali, Dar Abu Uma, and so forth
Box 4:
  File 38—Letters; for instance, one from Eduard Flegel on his plans for the exploration of Central Africa
Box 6:
  File 42—Arabic manuscripts from Wadai
Box 10:
  File 8—Original diary from Bornu
  File 15—Papers on Kanem
  File 16—Papers on Bagirmi

[4] Gustav Nachtigal, *Sahara und Sudan: Ergebnisse sechsjähriger Reisen in Afrika,* 3 vols. (vols. 1 and 2, Berlin: Weidmann, Parey 1879–81; vol. 3, Leipzig: Brockhaus 1889. The third volume on Wadai and Darfur was edited posthumously by E. Groddeck. All 3 volumes were reprinted in 1967 by Akademische Druck- und Verlagsanstalt, Graz. An English translation was published and annotated in Allan G. B. Fisher and Humphrey J. Fisher, trans., *Sahara and Sudan,* 4 vols. (London: Hurst 1971–87).

File 20—Various notes dating from 1871–73; namely, notes on Wadai and Darfur

Box 14:

File 32—Lectures, essays, and manuscripts: "Old Darfor," "Bornu, Wadai, Darfor," "Lake Tsad," "The Sheikh of Bornu and His Court," "The King of Wadai and His Court," and so forth[5]

I took the following notes on the contents of some boxes, after consulting the relevant files:

Box 1, file 24:

Nachtigal's notes, written in extremely tiny, nearly illegible handwriting, often on small pieces of paper. Many notes are listings of settlements, along with the determination of their relative geographical location.

Box 1, file 25:

Handwritten manuscript on Darfur, 58 pages in length. I made a quick comparison with the published account in the third volume of *Sahara and Sudan,* using the reprint from 1967, and at a first glance, I could not identify identical text passages. This, however, cannot be considered a definite finding because a systematic comparison would need much more time. The manuscript contains descriptions of both topographical features of the landscape and river system and political and territorial organization. These include listings of *dar*s (regions, provinces) with *shartaya*s (districts) and *dimlijiya* (subdistrict below a *shartaya*), detailed right down to the *hakura*s (estates), with notes on their geographical location.[6]

Box 4, file 38:

The box contains letters to and from Nachtigal. Among others, there is a sixteen-page letter by Eduard Flegel entitled "Meine Pläne zur Erforschung von Central-Afrika und meine gegenwärtige Lage: Ein Aufruf an die Förderer und Freunde deutscher Afrikaforschung zunächst gerichtet an den Kanzler des Deutschen Kaisers Seine Durchlaucht Fürsten Otto von Bismarck Schönhausen" (My Plans for the Exploration of Central Africa and My Current Situation: An Appeal to the Promoters and Friends of a German

[5] For a bibliography of Nachtigal's publications, see H. Fisher and J.-P. Farruggia, "Bibliographie de Gustav Nachtigal," *Journal des Africanistes* 46, nos. 1–2 (1976): 216–23.

[6] See glossary in R. S. O'Fahey, *The Darfur Sultanate: A History* (London: Hurst, 2008) and the listings of administrative units in Adelberger, "Vom Sultanat," 186 ff.

Exploration of Africa, First of All Addressing the Chancellor of the German Kaiser, His Highness Otto von Bismarck Schönhausen).

The box further contains a 41-page manuscript by Gottlob Adolf Krause, "Zur Geschichte von Fesan und Tripoli in Afrika: Auszug aus einer bisher unveröffentlichten arabischen Handschrift welche sich in der öffentlichen Bibliothek in Valetta auf der Insel Malta befindet" (On the History of Fesan and Tripoli in Africa: Excerpts from a So-Far Unpublished Arabic Manuscript Kept at the Public Library in Valetta on the Island of Malta).[7]

Box 10, file 20:

Original diary, inscribed with the word "for" and written in incredibly tiny, barely legible, handwriting. Notes on *dar*s (e.g., Dar Tebella, Dar Kuli, Zamebaya, etc.) and their subdivisions; sketches with hairstyles; history of Darfur, parts 1–5; detailed notes on Jebel Marra, with description of wadis (rivers) and *dar*s (e.g., Rowenna, Dar Wenna, Dar Deriba); notes on the provinces (Dar el Gharb etc.), with a breakdown of settlements.

I was able to identify the following names which apparently refer to descent groups (*orrenga*) of the Fur:

Mundanga or Andunga (I was not certain of the spelling), Kotinga, Dadinga, Murge, Marhalfange, Selabanga, Kunjara, Kera, Joringa, and Erlinga.[8]

Moreover, I found four pages on small, blue sheets of paper entitled "Foranbele" (language of the Fur), with notes on such traditional titles and offices of the Fur Sultanat as *Iyakuri* (sultan's premier wife), *orrondulung* (majordomo of palace), or *korkoa* (royal guard). Nachtigal expounds on these titles in the third volume of *Sahara und Sudan.*[9]

There is a further manuscript on the history of Wadai.

It is a fascinating experience to hold in your hand the original diaries in which Gustav Nachtigal wrote down his observations about 140 years ago and carried them with him through the expanses of Sudanic Africa.

A major obstacle for the researcher is the handwriting of Nachtigal,

---

[7] Gottlob Adolf Krause, "Zur Geschichte von Fesan und Tripoli in Afrika: Auszug aus einer bisher unveröffentlichten arabischen Handschrift welche sich in der öffentlichen Bibliothek in Valetta auf der Insel Malta befindet," *Zeitschrift der Gesellschaft für Erdkunde zu Berlin* 13 (1878): 356–73.

[8] For a listing of the various descent groups of the Fur see Adelberger, "Vom Sultanat," 141 ff.

[9] Nachtigal, *Sahara und Sudan,* 3:418 ff.

which bordered on illegibility. In his essay "Dr. Gustav Nachtigals Westafrikafahrt," Jürgen Germer comments on this: "Die Frage, warum seine persönlichen Aufzeichnungen bisher nicht ausgewertet wurden, lässt sich auch relativ einfach beantworten: Ohne Einübung und eine gewisse Sachkenntnis ist seine extrem kleine Handschrift fast nicht zu lesen."[10]

Nachtigal's notes are often written in extremely tiny letters, some found on small pieces of paper, some in pencil paled by age. Thus, the research potential of the papers is difficult to assess.

However, it became easily apparent that Nachtigal wrote down a great deal of data in meticulous detail, and it is obvious that not every single detail entered the eventually published account.

[10] Jürgen Germer, "Dr. Gustav Nachtigals Westafrikafahrt," Gustav Nachtigal Papers, Staatsbibliothek Berlin, http://www.altmark-pur.eu/html/ gustavnachtigal_7.html. Translation: The question of why his personal notes have not been utilized so far may be answered with relative ease: without practice and a certain knowledge his extremely diminutive handwriting is barely legible.

ZĀR IN UPPER EGYPT: HANS ALEXANDER WINKLER'S FIELD NOTES FROM 1932

Richard Johan Natvig

During his 1932 fieldwork in Naj' al-Kīmān, near Qifṭ in Upper Egypt, the German historian of religions Hans Alexander Winkler (1900–1945) invited some *zār* singers (*Ẓârbeschwörerinnen*) to the house in which he was staying. The *shayka* (leader) of the *zār,* Jâmne (Yāmne), was a black Sudanese woman who had learned the *zār* songs from her mother, and she from her mother who had come to Qifṭ from the Sudan. Yāmne and her companions—her daughter Ṣabrimenno, as well as an elderly woman, Sa'īde, with her daughter—brought their instruments with them in a basket. Yāmne played the *ṭār mushalshal* (tambourine with jingles; known elsewhere in Egypt as *riqq*), while the others each played a *ṭār* (large frame drum), and she sang a verse which the others repeated, usually seven times for each verse. The whole sitting lasted four hours with breaks during which Winkler had them repeat the words, and he wrote down the texts of the songs. Later he went through the songs once more with Yāmne to check and interpret the texts.

Winkler described this event in his *Bauern zwischen Wasser und Wüste* (*Farmers Between Water and Desert,* 1934), and in a footnote he commented that he hoped to come back to these *zār* songs.[1] However, he

[1] Hans Alexander Winkler, *Bauern zwischen Wasser und Wüste: Volkskundlisches aus dem Dorfe Kimân in Oberägypten* (Stuttgart: Kohlhammer, 1934), 15–16. For information on *zār,* the reader may consult, in addition to other references in the present paper, the entry by A. Rouaud and Tiziana Battain in *Encyclopaedia of Islam* (*EI*), 2d ed., s.v. "*Zār.*" Winkler's

Islamic Africa, VOL. 1, NO. 1, 2010. ISSN 2154-0993. www.islamicafricajournal.org

seems never to have published them, and my efforts to find out what happened to these particular notes have been unsuccessful. In Hans Alexander Winkler's papers (now housed at UAT) there is no trace of Yāmne and her songs.[2] I have, however, found in one of his notebooks (apparently the only one that has been preserved from the 1932 fieldwork) a brief entry in Arabic on *zār* which includes a few short song texts. This text was written probably a bit earlier during his stay in Upper Egypt, as I will argue below. I shall present this text in translation with comments and explanations. But first a few words about Winkler.

Hans Alexander Winkler

Hans Alexander Winkler was born in Bremerhaven on February 14, 1900. He was educated at Tübingen University and received his promotion from Enno Littmann on the basis of his thesis "Über das Wesen und die Herkunft einiger muhammedanischer Zaubercharaktere" ("On the Nature and Origin of Some Muhammedan Magic Characters") in February 1925. Three years later he received his habilitation in comparative religion and was appointed assistant at the Oriental Seminar at Tübingen University, a position he lost in 1933 because of his former membership in the German Communist Party. In 1930 he published his revised habilitation thesis as *Siegel und Charaktere in der muhammedanischen Zauberei* (*Seals and Characters in the Muhammedan Magic*), and in 1931 he published his second book, *Salomo und die Ḳarīna: Eine orientalische Legende von der*

field notes from 1932 are found in the Hans Alexander Winkler archive in Universitätsarchiv Tübingen (hereafter cited as UAT), archive 555. For UAT 555, see http://www.uni-tuebingen.de/uat/prov/datei578.htm (downloaded February 12, 2010). Winkler's papers were presented to UAT in two turns, first by his second wife Hedwig Winkler (1910–91) in 1989, and then by her heirs in 1994–95. I wish to thank UAT for supplying me with an inventory of Winkler's papers and photocopies of the notebook as well as of other material in the archive's Winkler collection. Here and elsewhere, translations are my own unless otherwise indicated.

[2] By all appearances, then, Yāmne's songs have been lost. Curious, though, is Enno Littmann's remark five years after Winkler's death: "Es wäre zu wünschen, daß auch diese Texte veröffentlicht würden, da sie zur weiteren Kenntnis solcher Beschwörungen dienen können" (It is to be wished that these texts, too, were published, since they would serve to expand our knowledge of such incantations). Enno Littmann, *Arabische Geisterbeschwörungen aus Ägypten* (Leipzig: Harrassowitz, 1950), vii. Surely, Littmann knew that Winkler was dead, so did he know that these texts were secure somewhere, perhaps in the keeping of another scholar?

Bezwingung einer Kindbettdämonin durch einen heiligen Helden (*Solomon and the Qarīna: An Oriental Legend on the Defeat of a Childbed Demon by a Holy Hero*).[3]

In the spring of 1932 Winkler went to Egypt for the first time and spent two months in Naj' al-Kīmān, Upper Egypt. In 1934 this field trip resulted in the publication of *Bauern*. With his former research into Muslim magic, amulets, incantations, spirit, and spirit-possession beliefs, it is not surprising that Winkler should take some interest in the *zār* phenomenon. This interest obviously was encouraged by his former teacher and supervisor, Enno Littmann. During the field trip Winkler must have been sending reports to Littmann, and in a letter dated March 31, 1932, the latter wrote back: "Daß Sie nun in Kīmān einen so guten Boden für Ihre Tätigkeit gefunden haben, ist sehr schön. Sie werden schon vielerlei wichtiges Material mitbringen. Einige Zār-Texte habe ich vor zwanzig Jahren aufgezeichnet; sie stehen Ihnen gern zur Verfügung, wenn Sie die Ihren bearbeiten wollen. Zeichnen Sie nur alles auf, was Sie hören" (That you have found such a good ground for your work in Kīmān is wonderful. Surely, you will bring back all sorts of important material. Twenty years ago I wrote down some *zār* texts; they are at your disposal when you set about to work on those of your own. Just write down everything that you hear).[4]

In the following years, Winkler made further field trips to Upper Egypt. He published *Ägyptische Volkskunde* (*Egyptian Folklore*) and *Die reitenden Geister der Toten* (*The Riding Spirits of the Dead*), both in 1936, as well as some studies of Upper Egyptian rock drawings for the Egypt Exploration Society in London, in 1938–39. From 1939 to 1944 he was engaged in the German foreign services and appears not to have published anything for the remainder of his life. In May 1944 he learned that his son had deserted from the army. Apparently feeling dishonored, Winkler then signed up for frontline duty. He was killed in combat near Toruń, Poland, on January 20, 1945.[5]

---

[3] See Hans Alexander Winkler, "Über das Wesen und die Herkunft einiger muhammedanischer Zaubercharaktere" (Ph.D. diss., Tübingen University, 1925); *Siegel und Charaktere in der muhammedanischen Zauberei* (Berlin and Leipzig: Walter de Gruyter, 1930); and *Salomo und die Ḳarīna: Eine orientalische Legende von der Bezwingung einer Kindbettdämonin durch einen heiligen Helden* (Stuttgart: Kohlhammer, 1931).

[4] Winkler, *Bauern;* Letter from Littmann to Winkler, March 31, 1932, UAT 555/40.

[5] See Hans Alexander Winkler, *Ägyptische Volkskunde* (Kohlhammer: Stuttgart, 1936); *Die reitenden Geister der Toten* (Stuttgart: Kohlhammer, 1936), translated into English by Nicholas S. Hopkins as *Ghost Riders of Upper Egypt: A Study of Spirit Possession* (Cairo

Text on Zār in Winkler's Fieldwork Notebook

Winkler's first fieldwork in Upper Egypt took place from February to April, 1932. He first stopped for a couple of days in Mallawi (between Minya and Asyût), in order to acclimate himself. Then followed a few days in Asyût and Qena, with a brief visit in Luxor, before he established base in the small village of Naj' al-Kīmān, near Qifṭ (ancient Koptos), located between Qena and Qūṣ on the east bank of the Nile.[6] Here he stayed for eight weeks. The only notebook (UAT 555/184) preserved from this fieldwork consists of forty-nine text pages.[7] The first entry in the notebook is from Asyût, with no date. Except for one page with the place-name Mallawi, and a few pages without place-names, all the rest of the pages up to page 15 are localized to Asyût but undated. Then follow six undated pages with no locale specified, including pages 17–19, which contain the text on *zār.* Page 22 is localized to Kīmān, and page 24 is both localized and dated "Kīmān 21. Febr." The rest of the notebook seems to consist of notes from Kīmān only, and the last date noted is March 9, on page 39.[8]

The text on *zār* is in Arabic with romanized transliteration. Arabic writing appears on the left-hand side of the pages, and the transliterated text on the right-hand side of the pages (except on page 19 where there is space for the transliteration but where no text appears). The transliteration is in Winkler's hand, recognizable all through the notebook, whereas the Arabic writing is in a different, experienced clear hand which occurs in the book only in the Asyût pages and up to page 21, the final page before the Kīmān pages take over. My suggestion is therefore that Winkler was assisted in Asyût by an Egyptian who took down some notes for him in Ara-

---

and New York: American University in Cairo Press, 2009); *The Rock-Drawings of Southern Upper Egypt* (London: Oxford University Press, 1938–39), vols. 1–2. See also Horst Junginger, "Das tragische Leben von Hans Alexander Winkler (1900–1945) und seiner armenischen Frau Hayastan (1901–1937)," in *Bausteine zur Tübinger Universitätsgeschichte,* ed. Volker Schäfer (Tübingen: Universitätsarchiv Tübingen, 1995), 7:83–110; and also his "Ein Kapitel Religionswissenschaft während der NS-Zeit: Hans Alexander Winkler (1900–1945)," *Zeitschrift für Religionswissenschaft* 3, no. 2 (1995): 137–61.

[6] His visit in Luxor was brief and apparently unpleasant, as he found the city ruined by the tourist industry. Winkler described his first days and weeks in Egypt and his settling down in Kīmān in the first chapter of his *Bauern* and referred to this fieldwork again in his *Ägyptische Volkskunde*. See Winkler, *Bauern,* 1–8; and *Ägyptische Volkskunde,* 1.

[7] For more, please see Hans Alexander Winkler, Notebook, 1932, UAT 555/184.

[8] The pagination is mine and excludes blank pages.

bic. Who this writer was is impossible to say; it may have been a member of the Ḥasanayn ʻAlī family with whom he stayed. The head of this family, merchant Ḥasanayn ʻAlī, was the father of the scholar Fuad Hasanein Ali, who at the time was studying orientalism in Germany with Enno Littmann as his supervisor.[9] The *zār* text must be from not long before February 21, 1932, and most likely, then, from Asyût.

Text

إيضاح عن الظار[10] يعنى الجن
الظار هم خلق من خلق الله تعاله مكلفين بعبادت الله ومأمورين مثلنا بإتبا ع
شريعة سيدنا محمد وهم قسمان منهم الصالحين ومن هم الضارين للناس وهم
يسمون الشياطين ورئيسهم إبليس اللعين
أسماء الظار
زَدُوه رمْنَدَّ مَمَّه الصَعيدى المغربى وورد الجناين أسماء رجالهم
وأسماء الستات هم رَينَه. سَفِينه. بنت الملوك هذه أسماء الستات

طريقت لعبهم على الطبل
اولا يقعدو خمس نسوان فيهم واحده وهى رئيستهم تسما شيخت الظار
تكمله الظار
فتقعت[11] شيختهم فى الوسط والأربعه الثانيين بجوارها من الجمبين وتمسك
شيختهم طارا كبيرا عنهم وتطبل بصوت عالى على الطبل حتى المرأه إللى عليها
جن لازم يحضر فى الحال فيغنوا له مثل واحده عليها المغربى فتقعد فى الوسط
أمام شيختهم وتقول شيختهم المغربى على المغربى رايح وظاير النبى المغربى إللى
تونس بلاده والسويس منزله

[9] Winkler, *Bauern,* 5; and Fuad Hasanein Ali, *Ägyptische Volkslieder* (Stuttgart: Kohlhammer, 1934), 197.

[10] The text is from UAT 555/184, 17–19 (my pagination). Each of the six sections in the Arabic text corresponds to each of the six sections in my English translation (see below). For a complete transliteration, see the appendix (below). Winkler's assistant wrote ظار—*ẓār*, not زار—*zār,* which probably reflects local pronounciation: "Der Name *zār* wird wegen des folgenden *r* öfters *ẓār* ausgesprochen und dann mit ẓ geschrieben." See Littmann, *Arabische Geisterbeschwörungen,* iv. On the *z/ẓ* change in Egyptian colloquial Arabic, see also William H. Worrell, "The Consonants Z and Ẓ in Egyptian Colloquial Arabic," *Journal of the American Oriental Society* 34 (1915): 278–81.

[11] The term فتقعت (for فتقعد; from *qaʻada,* "to sit down") probably reflects the writer's dialect. See Tetsuo Nishio, *The Arabic Dialect of Qifṭ (Upper Egypt): Grammar and Classified Vocabulary* (Tokyo: Institute for the Study of Languages and Cultures of Asia and Africa, 1994), 30 (devoicing assimilation).

غناوه لرمند.
عنده ليله عندنه محضر أبعتوا
لمه فى المدام يحضر وكمان رمند
فى المدام يحضر

غناوه لورد الجناين
ورد ال... الجناين [12] يحضر[13] يعود
الجناين يبيسيه على وردى

غناوه لمرومه
ستى مرومه عجنو لك الحنيه يمرومه
يا ستى جبو لك الجهاز
هذه غناء الظار

Translation

Explaining the *Zār,* That Is, the Jinn

The *zār* are among the creations of God most High. They are obligated with the worship of God and instructed like us with following the way of our Lord Muhammad. They are divided into two groups, for there are among them the pious ones and the harmful ones. Among men they [i.e., the harmful ones] are known as the *shayāṭīn,* and their leader is Iblīs, the accursed one.

Names of the *Zār*

Zadūh, Rumnad, Mamma, al-Ṣaʿīdī, al-Maghrabī, and Ward al-Janāyin are names of their men. And names of their ladies are Rīna, Safīna, and Bint al-Mulūk; these are some names of the ladies.

How They Play the Drum

At first, five women sit down. One of them is their leader, and she is called *shaykhat al-zār.* Their *shaykha* sits down in the middle, and the other four next to her on both sides. Their *shaykha* takes a big frame drum (*ṭār*) and beats loudly on the drum until the jinn possessing a woman has

---

[12] Here the text indicates that a word was crossed out—probably the word الجناين, which came out wrong and made the writer start over again.

[13] The term يحضر was emended by me from يخضر.

to make its presence at once,[14] and then they sing for him. For example, a woman who is possessed by al-Maghrabī sits down in the center in front of their *shaykha,* and their *shaykha* says [sings]: "Al-Maghrabī! For al-Maghrabī, he traveled and visited the Prophet, al-Maghrabī! Tunis is his country, and Suez his home."

A Song for Rumnad
He is having a night celebration,
We are having a party.
They invited Mamma to the place.
Come, too, Rumnad! Come to the place!

A Song for Ward al-Janāyin
Ward al-Janāyin, come!
Come again, al-Janāyin,
O Yusīh, for my Ward!

A Song for Marūma
Lady Marūma, they have kneaded the henna for you!
O Marūma, O Lady, they have prepared the trousseau for you!
These are songs of the *zār.*

Comments

The *Zār* Spirits and Their Names

The term *zār* is used vernacularly for a specific category of spirits and for the ceremonies centering on these spirits. These ceremonies have as their primary aim appeasing and coming to terms with the *zār* spirits, not exorcism. The spirits are spoken of in respectful terms, for instance, as *Asyād* (Lords) or *Mashāyikh* (Masters). They are seldom referred to by insiders as "jinn." One of my informants, Shaykhat al-zār Umm Shawqī, whom I met in 1980 at Abū Ṭūwāla (located in the al-Sharqiyya governate in Lower Egypt) during my fieldwork, told me that the spirits are called *mashāyikh* and stated emphatically that they are *rūḥ* (spirit), not jinn or *'afrīt* (demon or ghost)! *Zār* spirits are conceived of as different from *jinn.* They are, it is true, capricious, vindictive, unruly, unpredictable, and dangerous and will, when provoked, take possession of a person and thereby

[14] Literally: "Until the woman who has a jinn, it has to make its presence at once."

cause illness, but they are not intrinsically evil or satanic, since basic to *zār* is the notion that it is possible to enter into a meaningful and fruitful relationship with the *zār* spirits which results in the spirits withdrawing the harm they have caused but not in their possession of the person. The possession of a *zār* spirit is turned into something positive, through the rituals in the *zār* ceremonies. Under the guidance of a ritual specialist, the *shaykhat al-zār,* an agreement is reached between the spirit and the possessed, with terms and conditions for both parties.[15]

In order to be able to deal with the *zār* spirits and respond to them adequately, it is important to know the name of the possessing spirit. Each *zār* spirit has its personality and characteristics, which are often reflected in their individual names. Thus, during ritual possession, the possessed person will act out the characteristics of the spirit in question: al-Ḥākim Bāshā will dress, act, and speak like a doctor; al-Khawāja may speak (or pretend to speak) a foreign language and drink wine, and so on.

On a different level, however, the names reflect, in many cases, the complex multiethnic and multilinguistic background of the *zār* and its complex history, where indigenous and foreign beliefs and ritual practices have blended and accommodated (and continue to do so) in a creative process to become Egyptian *zār,* Sudanese zār, Yemeni *zār,* and so forth, in their various regional and local manifestations such as Upper or Lower Egyptian *zār,* village *zār,* or *zār* of big cities like Cairo.[16] These processes can sometimes be seen echoed in ritual terminology, in songs, or in spirit names. Zadūh here is a case in point: I suggest that this spirit and its name have their roots in North and West Africa. The name is probably a variant of the *zār* spirit name Gāddôh, as in Sulṭān al-Gāddôh, or Ǧāddôh (Jāddūh), also called Sulṭān al-Kābīnēh, "Ruler of the Toilet," in

[15] See Richard Natvig, "Liminal Rites and Female Symbolism in the Egyptian *Zar* Possession Cult," *Numen* 35, no. 1 (1988): 57–68.

[16] On relations between the West and North African *bori* and the *zār,* see, for example, René Khoury, "Note sur l'origine du *zār* et ses rapports avec le *vaudou* haïtien," *Annales islamologiques* 24 (1988): 295–301; and Ehud Toledano, *As If Silent and Absent: Bonds of Enslavement in the Islamic Middle East* (New Haven, Conn., and London: Yale University Press, 2007). On links between *zār* in Egypt and Ethiopia, see Richard Natvig, "Oromos, Slaves, and the *Zar* Spirits: A Contribution to the History of the *Zar* Cult," *International Journal of African Historical Studies* 20, no. 4 (1987): 669–89; and Richard Natvig, "Some Notes on the History of the *Zar* Cult in Egypt," in *Women's Medicine: The* Zar-Bori *Cult in Africa and Beyond,* ed. I. M. Lewis, Ahmed Al-Safi, and Sayyid Hurreiz, 178–88 (Edinburgh: Edinburgh University Press, 1991).

Cairo.[17] He is, as signaled by his nickname, related to dirt, to the toilet, and so forth. In Egypt, the name version Zadūh is, as far as I know, attested only in Winkler's notebook. In North Africa, however, we find the same interchange between *z* and *g/ǧ/j* in the initial consonant in this spirit's name. For example, in Algeria a little over a hundred years ago a spirit was known as "*Djattou, djinn* des latrines."[18] Tremearne, writing about the spirit-possession cult known as *bori* in North Africa, described Jato as a disgusting spirit, dirtiest of all, who usually lives in the drain, or the *salanga* (cesspit, latrine), and sniffs dung.[19] In Morocco, Za'toût or Zattou, "israélite de race," also called "le maître des water-closets," was one of the spirits invoked in the 'Issāwiyya brotherhood, as reported by Brunel in 1926.[20] More recently, Maurice Welte writes about Sīdī Za'ṭūṭ in the Moroccan *gnāwa* possession cult.[21]

Another traveling spirit is *Rumnad,* whom I suggest must be the same as Rumnat in *zār* songs that Paul Kahle recorded in Luxor.[22] Rumnat/Rumnad seems to be a purely Upper Egyptian name form, since, to

---

[17] Rudolf Kriss and Hubert Kriss-Heinrich, *Volksglaube im Bereich des Islam,* vol. 2, *Amulette, Zauberformeln und Beschwörungen* (Wiesbaden: Harrassowitz, 1962), 157, 158, 162; and Muna Nabhan, *Der* Zār-*Kult in Ägypten: Rituelle Begegnung von Geist und Mensch, Ein Beispiel komplementärer Gläubigkeit* (Frankfurt am Main: Peter Lang, 1994), 264–65.

[18] J. B. Andrews, *Les Fontaines des génies (Seba Aioun): Croyances soudanaises à Alger* (Algiers: Jourdan, 1903), 24.

[19] A. J. N. Tremearne, *The Ban of the* Bori: *Demons and Demon-Dancing in West and North Africa* (London: Heath, Cranton, and Ouseley, 1914), 347–48. Gerda Sengers mentions the *zār* spirits Gado and Saliha, "associated with impurity, e.g. the toilet," in *Women and Demons: Cult Healing in Islamic Egypt* (Leiden: Brill, 2003), 105. Jato is also known in Northern Sudanese *zār;* see P. M. Constantinides, "Sickness and the Spirits: A Study of the *Zaar* Spirit-Possession Cult in the Northern Sudan" (Ph.D. diss., University of London, 1972), 334.

[20] René Brunel, *Essai sur la confrérie religieuse des 'Aîssâoûa au Maroc* (Paris: Libraire Orientaliste, 1926), 162.

[21] Frank Maurice Welte, *Der* Gnāwa-*Kult: Trancespiele, Geisterbeschwörung und Besessenheit in Marokko* (Frankfurt am Main: Peter Lang, 1990), 286. He also discusses a connection between Bāšā Za'ṭūṭ and the spirit Nigritu Jatu recorded by Viviana Pâques in Algeria (Viviana Pâques, *L'arbre cosmiques dans la pensée populaire et dans la vie quotidienne du nord-ouest Africain* [Paris: Université de Paris, 1964]), Edward Westermarck's *jâṭu* in Morocco (Edward Westermarck, *Ritual and Belief in Morocco* [London: Macmillan, 1926]), and Jean Rouch's Zatao among the Songhay (Jean Rouch, *La religion et la magie songhay* [Paris: Presses Universitaires de Paris, 1960]); see Welte, *Der* Gnāwa-*Kult,* 310–12.

[22] Paul Kahle, "*Zâr*-Beschwörungen in Egypten," *Der Islam* 3 (1912): 35n4, 36–37.

my knowledge, it is not attested anywhere else in Egyptian (or other) *zār.* Kahle suggested that Rumnat is the same spirit who in other sources is called Rūmī Nagdī, a name he thought could have come from *rūm nagd,* which he thought might be a folk etymological invention to explain the original *rumnat.* My suggestion, which does not contradict Kahle's hypothesis, is that Rumnad/Rumnat is a variant of the name of a spirit in Ethiopian *zār* called Rom Näddad, literally "flame from Rome," who, according to Simon D. Messing, is a Christian spirit.[23]

Mamma, paired with Rumnad in "A Song for Rumnad" (see above), can be traced back to the early part of nineteenth-century Ethiopia and is therefore one of the oldest-named *zār* spirits.[24] Apart from its recognition in Ethiopia and Egypt, this spirit is known in the Sudan as well as in the Arabian peninsula. Doreen Ingrams (in Aden) cites "Mumma" along with "Yusei," where Yusei most probably is the same as Yusīh in "A Song for Ward al-Janāyin" (see above).[25]

In Lower Egypt, the *zār* spirit al-Ṣa'īdī represents a Lower Egyptian stereotype of the Ṣa'īdī (Upper Egyptian). Thus, al-Ṣa'īdī will dress and speak like an Upper Egyptian and may perform the characteristic Upper Egyptian stick fencing, and his female counterpart, al-Ṣa'īdiyya, may carry a *qullah* (earthenware water jug; the famous produce of Qena, Upper Egypt) on her head. Al-Ṣa'īdī is also known as al-Ṣa'īdī Abū Danfa or, simply, as Abū Danfa. In Kahle's *zār* songs from Luxor, however, "Abu Danfōh" is described as one who is being brought by an Arab *jallāba* (slave dealer)—he has, in other words, been enslaved. Although the name was explained to Kahle to be Sudanese and the song was accompanied by a Sudanese beat (*daqqat al-sūdānī*), Kahle looked farther and carefully hinted at a possible Ethiopian connection by pointing to the Ethiopian name Damfo, which must be the same name.[26] The fact that there

[23] Simon D. Messing, "The Highland-Plateau Amhara of Ethiopia" (Ph.D. diss., University of Pennsylvania, 1957), 619. See also Michel Leiris, "Le culte des *zars* à Gondar," *Aethiopica* 2 (1934): 102; and Thomas Leiper Kane, *Amharic-English Dictionary* (Wiesbaden: Harrassowitz, 1990), 373.

[24] Natvig, "Oromos," 679–80.

[25] Doreen Ingrams, *A Survey of Social and Economic Conditions in the Aden Protectorate* (Asmara: Government Printer, British Administration, Eritrea, 1949), 59. Bertram Thomas (in Oman) mentions "Of Mamid," perhaps a variant of the name "Mamma," along with several other spirit names that can only be of Ethiopian origin; see his *Alarms and Excursions in Arabia* (London: Allen and Unwin, 1931), 262.

[26] Kahle, "*Zâr*-Beschwörungen," 25. See also Littmann, *Arabische Geisterbeschwörungen,* 48; and Tiziana Battain, "Le *zār:* Rituel de possession en Égypte: De la souffrance

is an Ethiopian *zār* spirit named Dânfâ[27] suggests that Kahle was on the right track. This, along with the information from Bertram Thomas of a *zār* spirit in Oman named Dumfur,[28] leads me to believe that the origin of this spirit, too, is Ethiopia and that he, as with Mamma and Rom Näd-dad/Rumnad, "migrated" with *zār* as it spread from Ethiopia to the countries around. Furthermore, he is called "al-Ṣa'īdī" not because he came from Upper Egypt, but because he came from *al-ṣa'īd* (upstream), one of the root meanings of the word. In Cairo, al-Ṣa'īdī is sometimes identified with al-Ṣulṭān al-Gāddōh.[29] Again, what these two have in common, although from Ethiopia and from West and North Africa, respectively, is that they probably both came to Lower Egypt via Upper Egypt.

Al-Maghrabī is described in songs as a pilgrim (see the text above and the comment below). According to Kriss and Kriss-Heinrich, Ṣulṭān al-Maġrībī is equated with the great Sufi saint and patron of the Islamic West, 'Abd al-Qādir al-Ğīlānī.[30] However, there is also 'Abd al-Salām al-Maghrabī in one of Littmann's texts, who may be the celebrated Moroccan saint 'Abd al-Salām al-Mashīsh al-Ḥasanī (d. 625/1227–28).[31]

The name of the last of the male *zār* spirits listed, Ward al-Janāyin, literally "Rose(s) of the Gardens," is unusual. The only other "Ward" known to me is the Cairene *zār* spirit Sulṭān al-Ward al Aḥmar, "Sulṭān of the Red Roses."[32] I shall discuss this spirit in connection with the song for him (see below). Ward al-Janāyin is invoked along with Yusīh. The name Yusīh may derive from the Coptic name Yôsê, that is, Yūsuf, or from the Ethiopian names Yasô, Yôsā, and Yôsê, alternative forms of Yashū' (Joshua), which would point to an Ethiopian origin for Yusīh as a *zār* spirit. In any

---

à l'accomplissement," (Ph.D. diss., École des Hautes Études en Sciences Sociale, Paris, 1997), 186.

27 Michel Leiris, "Un rite médico-magique éthiopien: Le jet du *danqârâ'*," *Aethiopica* 3 (1935): 61–74, 72.

28 Thomas, *Alarms,* 262. According to Constantinides, Abu Danfar belongs (in Omdurman *zār*) to the *Khawajāt zār*s and is described as "a pilot of a small boat"; Constantinides, "Sickness and the Spirits," 338.

29 Kriss and Kriss-Heinrich, *Volksglaube,* 2:157; see also Battain, "Le *zār,*" 186.

30 Kriss and Kriss-Heinrich, *Volksglaube,* 2:147; see also Battain, "Le *zār,*" 188.

31 Littmann, *Arabische Geisterbeschwörungen,* 36, 56; and Nabhan, *Der* Zār-*Kult,* 272. Although Littmann's *Arabische Geisterbeschwörungen* was published in 1950, it should be noted that the *zār* manuscripts that he translated and discussed in the book were written in Cairo in 1911 and 1930 but ultimately go back to Egyptian prints from 1903 and 1910, respectively; see *Arabische Geisterbeschwörungen,* iii–vi.

32 Kahle, "*Zâr*-Beschwörungen," 30. Probably not relevant here is Al Wardi Karoma = Lord Cromer, a *zār* spirit in Northern Sudan; see Constantinides, "Sickness and the Spirits," 338.

case, he is closely related to Mamma, as his son or his deputy.[33] "Yusei," mentioned by Doreen Ingrams along with "Mumma," in Aden, is probably the same as Yusīh here.[34]

The female spirits Rīna and Safīna, as well as Marūma (diminutive of Maryam) in "A Song for Marūma" (see above), are all old and well-known spirits in Egyptian *zār.* Rīna is thought of as an Ethiopian and, according to Battain, as the sister of Ğaddôh, whereas Nabhan's informants variously called her Ethiopian and Sudanese. Rīna is, however, also the name of a female spirit in the Moroccan *gnāwa* possession cult.[35] Safīna (literally "ship") is related to the Nile and its waters, and is well known in Upper and Lower Egypt, as well as in the Sudan. She is described as a mermaid who has a woman's upper body and a fish's tail.[36] Marūma is an Ethiopian, daughter of Mamma, the sister of Rūmī Nagdī.[37] In one of Kahle's song texts from Cairo, she is called "*eṣ-ṣa'īdîjə,*" which probably should not be taken literally, as "aus Oberägypten,"[38] but as meaning "from upstream" or "from far away (in the south)." The name Bint al-Mulūk, (the Rulers' Daughter) may be the same as Muna Nabhan's al-Baiḍa al-Bint al-Mulūk, a child spirit counted as one of the Mulūk al-Arḍiyya (Rulers of the Earth/(Under)ground).[39]

Summoning the *Zār* Spirits

A person who has become possessed by a *zār* spirit is not believed to be in a state of constant possession after the spirit has been appeased. She (or he) "*has* a spirit," *'alayha al-zār,* and as long as the agreed-upon terms are respected, it is in the ritual contexts only that the spirit will (re-)appear and (re-)take control of the possessed person. The drumbeat is what makes the

[33] Littmann, *Arabische Geisterbeschwörungen,* 52; Battain, "Le *zār,*" 182.

[34] Ingrams, *Survey,* 59.

[35] Battain, "Le *zār,*" 192; Nabhan, *Der* Zār-*Kult,* 265; Welte, *Der* Gnāwa-*Kult,* 307–8.

[36] Littmann, *Arabische Geisterbeschwörungen,* 2, 7, 14, 18, 31, 36, 55, 66, 69, 70 passim; Kahle, "*Zâr*-Beschwörungen," 28–29; Nabhan, *Der* Zār-*Kult,* 67, 179, 263; Constantinides, "Sickness and the Spirits," 337; Battain, "Le *zār,*" 191–92, 414–15; Kriss and Kriss-Heinrich, *Volksglaube,* 2:147 passim, illustrations on 118–20.

[37] Littmann, *Arabische Geisterbeschwörungen,* 13, 52, 69; Sengers, *Women and Demons,* 104; Kahle, "*Zâr*-Beschwörungen," 26, 27, 29; Kriss and Kriss-Heinrich, *Volksglaube,* 2:146.

[38] Kahle, "*Zâr*-Beschwörungen," 29.

[39] Nabhan, *Der* Zār-*Kult,* 266.

spirit come and enter the person's body. When the spirit has entered the body, the possessed *is* the spirit, the words of the song are directed to the possessing spirit, and the person's actions are those of the spirit.

Each spirit not only has a certain beat which attracts it and makes it appear in the ceremony but also has songs that address each one in particular. The first song, or excerpt of a song, calling on al-Maghrabī and characterizing him as a pious Muslim ("Al-Maghrabī! For al-Maghrabī, he traveled and visited the Prophet, al-Maghrabī!" [see above]), has parallels in the literature on *zār*. For example, Galal cites the following: "Rayeḥ fen ya maġrâbey? Râyeḥ makka w'elḥaram ennabey" (Where are you going, o Maghrabī? You are going to Mecca and the Prophet's mosque).[40] The line "Tunis is his country, and Suez his home" (see above) should not be taken literally. It is an idiomatic expression which characterizes al-Maghrabī as widely traveled. Again, parallels can be found in other songs: "Mekka bilāādêê wil-ḥabaš manzalêê" (Mecca is my country, and Abyssinia is my home).[41]

The second song, inviting Mamma and Rumnad to the night celebration (i.e., the *zār* ceremony) and to the place (*mīdām,* from *mīdān;* i.e., the ritual space), can be compared with songs Kahle recorded in Cairo and Luxor. Such songs include the song from Cairo: "'andinā lêle ulêle 'andinā, [. . .] jeḥḍar 'andinā sulṭân mama, fī 'l-mīdân jeḥḍar 'andinā, [. . .] jeḥḍar 'andinā rûmī nagdī (We are having a night celebration, and the night celebration is with us, [. . .] come to us, Sulṭān Mamma, come to us to the place, [. . .] come to us, Rūmī Nagdī)." A further example is the following song from Luxor: "Mama nizil el-mudân [mīdān], [. . .] rumnat nizil el-mudân, [. . .] josê nizil el-mudân (Mamma descend to the place, [. . .] Rumnat descend to the place, [. . .] Yusīh descend to the place."[42]

---

40 "Où vas-tu, O mograbin? Tu vas à la Mecque et à la mosquée du Prophète." See Mohammed Galal, "Essai d'observations sur les rites funéraires en Égypte actuelle," *Revue des études islamiques* 2, nos. 2–3 (1937): 132–299, 149. Compare also Littmann, *Arabische Geisterbeschwörungen,* 22, 27–28.

41 Littmann, *Arabische Geisterbeschwörungen,* 13, 99; see also Battain, "Le *zār,*" 417. My interpretation here relies on Heinrich Schäfer. He translated "*Mikke bilādi, wel ḥabaš manzali*" as "Mekka ist mein Heimatsland und Abessinien mein Wohnort" (Mecca is my country, and Abyssinia is my home) but explained it to mean (in the context): "Ich bin ein weitgereister großer Mann" (I am a well-traveled, important man). See Heinrich Schäfer, *Die Lieder eines ägyptischen Bauern* (Leipzig: J. C. Hinrichs'sche Buchandlung, 1903), 60.

42 Kahle, "*Zâr*-Beschwörungen," 16, 35. That Rumnat and Mamma are invoked together in the Luxor song, just as Rūmī Nagdī and Mamma are invoked together in the Cairo song,

The third song (see above) calls on Ward al-Janāyin and Yusīh, Mamma's son or deputy: "Ward al-Janāyin, come! Come again, al-Janāyin, O Yusīh, for my Ward!" The identity of Ward al-Janāyin is unknown. The pairing of him with Yusīh in this song may, however, be a clue: Sengers mentions Warayid as the brother of Yusīh.[43] Warāyid, etymologically, must be related to Ward,[44] so could Ward al-Janāyin be identical to Warāyid, that is, the brother of Yusīh?

The song invoking Marūma is interesting for its use of wedding metaphors: the henna that has been kneaded—that is, ready to be applied—and Marūma's trousseau (bride's outfit) that has been prepared. In the above song, Marūma, or the possessed person, is being prepared for marriage. In Egypt, basically two kinds of *zār* ceremonies are held: a weekly ceremony that consists of music, songs, and dancing in ritual possession and an annual ceremony that is held especially for one particular possessed person (or several persons), during which time this person (or persons) fulfills her/his (or their) obligations towards the spirit. This annual ceremony includes (in addition to music) songs, dancing, sacrifices, and meals. During this ceremony (sometimes called *faraḥ ma'a al-asyād* [wedding with the masters]), the ritual subject, called *'arūsat al-zār* (*zār* bride), is prepared for the ceremony like a bride. This wedding ceremony includes the ceremony known as *leilat al-ḥinnā'* (henna evening), when the ritual subject cleans and grooms herself and applies henna to her hands and feet. She then dresses in a new clean dress—either in white, like a bride, or in a color specifically ordered by her spirit (husband)—and she adorns herself with jewelry and amulets, getting ready for the *faraḥ*.[45] Thus, this song refers explicitly to the marital union which will take place between the possessed and her *zār* spirit, Marūma.

Concluding Comments: Upper Egypt and the Zār

The earliest certain report on *zār* in Egypt comes from Upper Egypt. Carl Benjamin Klunzinger, who had been based as a quarantine doctor in Quṣayr on the Upper Egyptian Red Sea coast in the years 1863–69 and 1872–75, wrote in his book *Bilder aus Oberägypten* (*Scenes from Upper*

strengthens the suggestion that Rumnat/Rumnad and Rūmī Nagdī may be the same spirit; see the discussion above.

[43] Sengers, *Women and Demons,* 104.

[44] Littmann, *Arabische Geisterbeschwörungen,* 65.

[45] For a full discussion, see Natvig, "Liminal Rites."

Egypt; published in 1877) that women "haben sich ein durch, wie man sagt, abyssinische Sklavinnen eingeschlepptes Mittel [*zār*] adoptirt, das nach und nach so einriss, dass die Regierung sich veranlasst fühlte, es zu verbieten. Nichts desto weniger ist es noch allgemein bei Hoch und Nieder, *zumal in Oberägypten,* im Schwang" ("have adopted a practice [zār] which is said to have been introduced by Abyssinian female slaves, and which gradually spread to such an extent that the government felt itself called upon to forbid it. Nevertheless, it is still common among high and low, *especially in Upper Egypt*" [my emphasis]).[46] Thirty-five years later, Klunzinger's claim that the *zār* was especially popular in Upper Egypt was confirmed by Paul Kahle, who wrote that he had the impression that *zār* was more widespread the further south one traveled in Egypt.[47]

Almost all research on *zār* in Egypt has focused on Lower Egypt, and predominantly on *zār* in Cairo. In comparison, the number of research publications on Upper Egyptian *zār* is almost negligible. In addition to the limited descriptions in Hans Alexander Winkler's publications, there are only Paul Kahle's article "Zâr-Beschwörungen in Egypten," which includes the only published collection of *zār* songs from Upper Egypt (Luxor), and the British ethnographer Winifred S. Blackman's few pages describing the *zār* in her *The Fellahin of Upper Egypt,* based on her fieldwork in the Asyût region and in the Fayyūm, especially in and around al-Lāhūn, in the 1920s.[48]

---

[46] C. B. Klunzinger, *Bilder aus Oberägypten: Der Wüste und dem Rothen Meere* (Stuttgart: Levy and Müller, 1877), 388; English quotation is from the translation, *Upper Egypt: Its People and Products* (London: Blackie and Son, 1878), 395. Another early but brief mention of *zār* in Upper Egypt (Aswân) is Lucie Duff Gordon's side remark in a letter to her husband: "Ask any learned pundit to explain to you the *Sar*—it is really curious." See her letter dated January 25, 1869, in Lucie Duff Gordon, *Lady Duff Gordon's Letters from Egypt,* 3d ed., rev. by Janet Ross (1902; repr., London: Virago, 1983), 309 (citation is to reprint). For a discussion of early sources on *zār* in Egypt, see Natvig, "Some Notes."

[47] Kahle, "*Zâr*-Beschwörungen," 6. See also William H. Worrell, who notes that it is "the Zar, which seems to be more cultivated in upper than in lower Egypt, and therefore to have come down the Nile and not across from Mecca by the pilgrim route" ("The Demon of Noonday and Some Related Ideas," *Journal of the American Oriental Society* 38 [1918]: 160–66, 165).

[48] Winifred S. Blackman, *The Fellahin of Upper Egypt* (1927; new impression, London: Frank Cass, 1968), 198–200. In addition to the literature mentioned above, *zār* in a village across the Nile from Luxor was described in a short paper by W. Benson Harer, Jr., "Azarr: A Spirit of Women's Liberation, Rural Egyptian Style," *American Research Center in Egypt Newsletter* 123 (Fall 1983): 35–38. There is also a short description in Omm Sety [*Dorothy Louise Eadon*], *Omm Sety's Living Egypt: Surviving Folkways from Pharaonic Times,*

Upper Egypt may very well have played a more important role in the early history and dissemination of *zār* in Egypt than is realized today. Asyût, Qena, Quṣayr, and Aswân were all, in the period when *zār* in Egypt "indigenized" and became Egyptian *zār* (i.e., in the course of the nineteenth century),[49] still very important centers of trade, both short and long distance, including the still considerable trade in slaves. They were bustling centers and junctions for pilgrims to and from Mecca, for other travelers from West and Northwest Africa, and for the Sudan and countries beyond the Sudan; they were meeting grounds for city dwellers and Fellahin and Bedouins. And where people meet, ideas, beliefs, and religious practices meet and are exchanged. It may be significant that the *zār* spirits Zadūh and Rumnad carry their names in forms different from the Lower Egyptian versions—forms, that is, that seem to point to North and West Africa and Ethiopia, respectively. It may also be significant that spirits whose roots can be traced from further away, Ethiopia or West Africa, yet in Lower Egypt, are characterized as *ṣa'īdī* or *ṣa'īdiyya.* This may suggest that Lower Egypt came to know these spirits from Upper Egypt. Then, too, in view of Klunzinger's and Kahle's observations on *zār* in Upper Egypt, there is every reason to regret that so little has been researched and published on *zār* in these parts.

Appendix
Winkler's Transliteration of the *Zār* Text

iḍah an ẓār jānī eğğinn

aẓzār hum ḫalg min ḫalg allah ta'āla mukallafīm bi'ibādāt illāh wa ma'mūrīn mitlanā bitba' šarī'a saijidinā muḥammad wahum ḳismān minhum al-ṣāliḥīn waminhum eḍ-ḍārrīn. linnās wahum isamūna aššaijāṭīn waraisuhum iblis al-la'īn.

ed. Nicole B. Hansen (Chicago: Glyphdoctors, 2008), 65–67; and there are the briefest mentions of *zār* in various books and papers. Most of this literature is, however, of little value other than as a testimony that the *zār* existed in Upper Egypt at the time of the observation. Nubian *zār* has not been much researched, either. John G. Kennedy's "Nubian *Zar* Ceremonies as Psychotherapy," in *Human Organization* 24, no. 4 (1967): 185–94, augmented for the volume he edited in 1978, John G. Kennedy, ed., *Nubian Ceremonial Life: Studies in Islamic Syncretism and Cultural Change* (Berkeley: University of California Press 1978), 203–23, is just about all that has been published on *zār* among Egyptian Nubians.

[49] See Natvig, "Some Notes."

asmā' aẓẓār
zadoh rumnad mama aṣṣa'īdī, al-maġrabī ward il-ğanājin asmā riğālhum.
wi asmā assittāthum rīna, safīna, bint il-mulūk, hādihī asmā assittāt.

ṭarīka la'bukum alai al-ṭabl
auwalan jaḳ'udu ḫamas niswān fihum waḥida ra'isatahum tusamma schech[e] t aẓẓār.
takmilat aẓẓār. [fa]taḳ'ud šeḫethum fil wasṭ welarb'a aṯṯānija biğawārihā min alğambain wetamsik šeḫethum ṭāran kabīran 'anhum wetuṭṭabil biṣōt 'alī 'alā aṭ-ṭabl ḥatta al-mar'a illi 'aleihā ğinn lāzim jiḥ-[letters crossed out]-ḍar fi'l-ḥāl fajurannu [*sic,* for *fajuġannu*] lahu miṯla wāḥida 'aleiha al-maġrabī fata'ḳud [*sic,* for fataḳ'ud] filwaṣt amām šeḫethum watgūl šeḫethum al-maġrabī 'ala al-maġrabī rā'iḥ waẓā'ir linnabī [*sic,* for innabī] el-maġrabī [il]lī tuns bilādu wi lsu'es manzalu

ġunā lirumnad
'indinā leila 'inda maḥḍar[50] ib'atu limama fi 'l mudām jiḥḍar ukamān rumnad fi 'l-mudām jiḥdar

[Page 19]
ġunā liward il-ğanājin
Ward il-ğanājin jiḫḍar ji'ūd il-ğanājin jajusēh 'alā wardī.

ġunā limarōma
sittī marōma 'ağanū laki 'lḥinaja jamarōma jā sittī ğabbū laki 'l-ğihāz
hāḏihi ġunā' aẓẓār

50 In transliterating "*'indinā leila 'inda maḥḍar,*" Winkler reversed the word order. The Arabic text goes "*'indah leila 'indinā maḥḍar.*" The last page (page 19) was not transliterated by Winkler. I have transliterated the last page of the Arabic text following his system. For the full Arabic text and my translation, see above.

Bibliography

ʻAlī, Fu'ād Ḥasanein. *Ägyptische Volkslieder.* Stuttgart: Kohlhammer, 1934.

Andrews, J. B. *Les Fontaines des génies (Seba Aioun): Croyances soudanaises à Alger.* Algiers: Jourdan, 1903.

Battain, Tiziana. "Le *zār:* Rituel de possession en Égypte: De la souffrance à l'accomplissement." Ph.D. diss., École des Hautes Études en Sciences Sociale, Paris, 1997.

Benson Harer, Jr., W. "Azarr; A Spirit of Women's Liberation, Rural Egyptian Style." *American Research Center in Egypt, Newsletter* 123 (Fall 1983): 35–38.

Blackman, Winifred S. *The Fellahin of Upper Egypt.* 1927. New impression, London: Frank Cass, 1968.

Brunel, René. *Essai sur la confrérie religieuse des 'Aîssâoûa au Maroc.* Paris: Libraire Orientaliste, 1926.

Constantinides, P.M. "Sickness and the Spirits: A Study of the *Zaar* Spirit-Possession Cult in the Northern Sudan." Ph.D. diss., University of London, 1972.

Duff Gordon, Lucie. *Lady Duff Gordon's Letters from Egypt.* Revised by Janet Ross. 1902. 3d reprint, London: Virago, 1983.

Galal, Mohammed. "Essai d'observations sur les rites funéraires en Égypte actuelle." *Revue des études islamiques* 2, nos. 2–3 (1937): 132–299.

Ingrams, Doreen. *A Survey of Social and Economic Conditions in the Aden Protectorate.* Asmara: Government Printer, British Administration, Eritrea, 1949.

Junginger, Horst. "Das tragische Leben von Hans Alexander Winkler (1900–1945) und seiner armenischen Frau Hayastan (1901–1937)." In *Bausteine zur Tübinger Universitätsgeschichte,* edited by Volker Schäfer, 7:83–110. Tübingen: Universitätarchiv Tübingen, 1995.

———. "Ein Kapitel Religionswissenschaft während der NS-Zeit: Hans Alexander Winkler (1900–1945)." *Zeitschrift für Religionswissenschaft* 3, no. 2 (1995): 137–61.

Kahle, Paul. "*Zâr*-Beschwörungen in Egypten." *Der Islam* 3 (1912): 1–41.

Kane, Thomas Leiper. *Amharic-English Dictionary.* Wiesbaden: Harrassowitz, 1990.

Kennedy, John G. "Nubian *Zar* Ceremonies as Psychotherapy." *Human Organization* 26, no. 4 (1967): 185–94. Augmented in John G. Kennedy, ed. *Nubian Ceremonial Life: Studies in Islamic Syncretism and Cultural Change.* Berkeley: University of California Press, 1978.

Khoury, René. "Note sur l'origine du *zār* et ses rapports avec le *vaudou* haïtien." *Annales islamologiques* 24 (1988): 295–301.

Klunzinger, C. B. *Bilder aus Oberägypten, der Wüste und dem Rothen Meere.* Stuttgart: Levy and Müller, 1877.

Kriss, Rudolf, and Hubert Kriss-Heinrich. *Volksglaube im Bereich des Islam.* Vol. 2, *Amulette, Zauberformeln und Beschwörungen.* Wiesbaden: Harrassowitz, 1962.

Leiris, Michel. "Le culte des *zars* à Gondar." *Aethiopica* 2 (1934): 96–103, 125–36.

———. "Un rite médico-magique éthiopien: Le jet du *danqârâ*." *Aethiopica* 3 (1935): 61–74.

Littmann, Enno. *Arabische Geisterbeschwörungen aus Ägypten.* Leipzig: Harrassowitz, 1950.

Messing, Simon D. "The Highland-Plateau Amhara of Ethiopia." Ph.D. diss., University of Pennsylvania, 1957.

Nabhan, Muna. *Der* Zār-*Kult in Ägypten: Rituelle Begegnung von Geist und Mensch, Ein Beispiel komplementärer Gläubigkeit.* Frankfurt am Main: Peter Lang, 1994.

Natvig, Richard. "Liminal Rites and Female Symbolism in the Egyptian *Zar* Possession Cult." *Numen* 35, no. 1 (1988): 57–68.

———. "Oromos, Slaves, and the *Zar* Spirits: A Contribution to the History of the *Zar* Cult." *International Journal of African Historical Studies* 20, no. 4 (1987): 669–89.

———. "Some Notes on the History of the *Zar* Cult in Egypt." In *Women's Medicine: The* Zar-Bori *Cult in Africa and Beyond,* edited by I. M. Lewis, Ahmed Al-Safi, and Sayyid Hurreiz, 178–88. Edinburgh: Edinburgh University Press, 1991.

Nishio, Tetsuo. *The Arabic Dialect of Qifṭ (Upper Egypt): Grammar and Classified Vocabulary.* Tokyo: Institute for the Study of Languages and Cultures of Asia and Africa, 1994.

Pâques, Viviana. *L'arbre cosmiques dans la pensée populaire et dans la vie quotidienne du nord-ouest Africain.* Paris: Université de Paris, 1964.

Rouch, Jean. *La religion et la magie songhay.* Paris: Presses Universitaires de Paris, 1960.

Schäfer, Heinrich. *Die Lieder eines ägyptischen Bauern.* Leipzig: J. C. Hinrichs'sche Buchandlung, 1903.

Sengers, Gerda. *Women and Demons: Cult Healing in Islamic Egypt.* Leiden: Brill, 2003.

Sety, Omm [Dorothy Louise Eadon]. *Omm Sety's Living Egypt: Surviving Folk-*

ways from Pharaonic Times. Edited by Nicole B. Hansen. Chicago: Glyphdoctors, 2008.

Thomas, Bertram. *Alarms and Excursions in Arabia.* London: Allen and Unwin, 1931.

Toledano, Ehud R. *As If Silent and Absent: Bonds of Enslavement in the Islamic Middle East.* New Haven, Conn., and London, 2007.

Tremearne, A. J. N. *The Ban of the* Bori: *Demons and Demon-Dancing in West and North Africa.* London: Heath, Cranton, and Ouseley, 1914.

Welte, Frank Maurice. *Der* Gnāwa-*Kult: Trancespiele, Geisterbeschwörung und Besessenheit in Marokko.* Frankfurt am Main: Peter Lang, 1990.

Westermarck, Edward. *Ritual and Belief in Morocco.* 2 vols. London: Macmillan, 1926.

Winkler, Hans Alexander. *Ägyptische Volkskunde.* Stuttgart: Kohlhammer, 1936.

———. *Bauern zwischen Wasser und Wüste: Volkskundlisches aus dem Dorfe Kimân in Oberägypten.* Stuttgart: Kohlhammer, 1934.

———. *Die reitenden Geister der Toten.* Stuttgart: Kohlhammer, 1936. Translated by Nicholas S. Hopkins as *Ghost Riders of Upper Egypt: A Study of Spirit Possession.* Cairo and New York: American University in Cairo Press, 2009.

———. *The Rock-Drawings of Southern Upper Egypt.* 2 vols. London: Oxford University Press, 1938–39.

———. *Salomo und die Ḳarīna: Eine orientalische Legende von der Bezwingung einer Kindbettdämonin durch einen heiligen Helden.* Stuttgart: Kohlhammer, 1931.

———. *Siegel und Charaktere in der muhammedanischen Zauberei.* Berlin and Leipzig: Walter de Gruyter, 1930.

Worrell, William H. "The Consonants Z and Ẓ in Egyptian Colloquial Arabic." *Journal of the American Oriental Society* 34 (1915): 278–81.

———. "The Demon of Noonday and Some Related Ideas." *Journal of the American Oriental Society* 38 (1918): 160–66.

Archival Material

Winkler, Hans Alexander (1900–1945). Nachlaß, 1900–1982. UAT, Bestandsignatur 555. http://www.uni-tuebingen.de/uat/prov/datei578.htm (downloaded February 12, 2010).

THERE ONCE WAS A MAN: A REVIEW

Madia Thomson

Virtually no studies exist on Berber culture and society in English; studies of the Berber language in English are even rarer. This comes as no surprise when one considers that France either colonized (Algeria), invaded (Egypt), or made a protectorate (Morocco) of every country with a Berber-speaking population, making French the principal language of Berber studies. In the course of their conquests, however, French officials made a point of documenting the 'manners and customs' of their subjects. In the nineteenth century in particular, Berber life became the source of great debate and mythology both within the community of Europeans who went to North Africa and those who lived in the metropole.

Not to be outdonc by continental language speakers, English speakers also joined the fray with greater intensity. Debates and dissertations on Berber culture and society appeared in the newly independent United States, as members of the American Philosophical Society considered the implications of European colonization and what it meant for the study of foreign cultures. Like their European counterparts, members of the Philosophical Society who met in Philadelphia wondered about Berber identity and origins. By the late nineteenth century, however, this scholarly debate had begun to fade in the United States. Europeans would continue the discussion amongst themselves and those who lived in the countries subject to their colonial authority. French scholarship remains the point of reference for such discussions. For the small and (hopefully) growing community of people interested in Berber studies who do not read

Islamic Africa, VOL. 1, NO. 1, 2010. ISSN 2154-0993. www.islamicafricajournal.org

French, however, there is Harry Stroomer's *Tashelhiyt Berber Folktales from Tazerwalt (South Morocco)*, volume four of the Rüdiger Köppe Berber Studies Series.[1] There is much to learn in spite of the "south" rather than "southern" in the title.

A History

The first English-language translation of Hans Stumme's *Märchen der Schluḥ von Tázerwalt,*[2] Harry Stroomer's *Tashelhiyt Berber Folktales,* begins with an introduction that includes a short biographical sketch of Hans Stumme. One learns that Stumme's linguistic studies at Leipzig University included languages from the Hamitic, Semitic, and Ugaritic families and that it was during this period prior to his actual employment in Leipzig in 1895 that he made a "multicountry trip" that included a visit to North Africa. Unfortunately for the reader, however, Stroomer seems to have written this section a bit too quickly, without considering the importance of chronology and historical sequence to comprehension. He mentions the trip on page 16, and then, after much intervening detail, one learns on page 17 that Stumme actually studied Tachelhit Berber in Tunis in 1889. One does not know whether Stumme left Germany in 1887 and stayed away for two years during which time he went to Tunisia, or if the multicountry trip was really a series of shorter trips taken over the course of two years. That the information appears in a quote with no apparent connection to the paragraph that precedes it or the section that follows it only complicates matters. These difficulties aside, however, the detail on education is quite useful as it gives a sense of what was possible for a well-schooled person in Africa or Europe during the years immediately following the Berlin Conference (1884–85).[3] Europeans of all sorts had traveled to the Maghreb by 1889, and France had clearly established herself as an occupying force in both Algeria and Tunisia. As one would see again with the establishment of the Protectorate in Morocco, French officials often sent

---

[1] Harry Stroomer, *Tashelhiyt Berber Folktales fromTazerwalt (South Morocco),* Berber Studies (Cologne: Rüdiger Köppe Verlag, 2002). I forgot to mention in the text that the subtitle appears on the website but does not appear on the cover of the book. It only appears on the title page.

[2] Hans Stumme, *Märchen der Schluḥ von Tázerwalt* (Leipzig: J. C. Hinrichs, 1895).

[3] The Berlin Conference established the general principles for late nineteenth-century imperial expansion. Representatives from all the major imperial powers in Europe and Asia attended.

established members of their colonial administration to their new territories. Officers who had served in Algeria or Vietnam might be sent to other colonies in North or West Africa as was the case with Louis Lyautey, the first résident-général of Morocco, and his successor, Theódore Steeg. That Stumme could study Tachelhit in Tunisia suggests that someone, either official or unofficial, French or not, had been able to learn the language well enough to offer a course to a traveling student in Tunis. Though it has the basic elements for one, the biographical section of the introduction lacks the requisite attention to chronology and narrative sequence that would make it a strong opening to an important translation.

In addition to the information about Stumme's schooling, the introduction includes a "quote" from Stumme about how he got the stories. Stroomer writes that Hans Stumme met his informant, Haj Abdalla ben Muhammed, in Stockholm, where the latter was performing with a troupe of acrobats in 1894. On the basis of what we know of Tazerwalt, he was probably traveling with the Ramiyat, a group of acrobat athletes associated with a religious center, the zawiya of Sidi Ahmed ou Moussa, in Tazerwalt. The name Sîdî Aḥmad ou Mûsâ actually appears in some of the stories and refers to the saint (d. 1563) who founded the zawiya in southwestern Morocco in the sixteenth century.[4] Stroomer mentions nothing about how Stumme got to Stockholm or about what happened to Haj Abdallah ben Muhammed after this meeting. This is obviously not the purpose of the book, but, as with more attention to narrative sequence, its addition would greatly improve the quality of the introduction.

The Process of Translation

Stroomer also uses the introduction to discuss his changes to the translated stories, which are impressively clear in both English and Tachelhit despite the many stages of telling, translation, and transliteration they necessarily underwent before getting a clean English version. As mentioned earlier, Hans Stumme studied Tachelhit in Tunisia in 1889 and was collecting stories in Tachelhit after only five years of intermittent study. He wrote the tales in Tachelhit, transliterated them using German phonetics, then translated them into German. This is an impressive feat by any measure, and

[4] For a short summary of the life of Sidi Ahmed ou Moussa, see Madia Thomson, "*Tikettan yat famila*/Once upon a Family: Family Origins and Slave Histories in Southern Morocco," *African Diaspora Archaeology Network Newsletter* (December 2006).

Table 1

Problem	Stumme	Stroomer	Translation
Gemination	lkyst **nlahtab**	lqist **nlhttab**	the story of the woodcutter
Velarisation	**arsbah**	**ar sbah**	until the morning
Annexed state	**htigimenu**	**x tgmmi nu**	at my house

the sense of it is merely heightened by Stroomer's discussion of his corrections to the text. Concerned about Stumme's transliterations, Stroomer first rewrote them, then translated them into English. Table 1 gives a sense of the kind of changes Stroomer made.

As Table 1 shows, Stroomer's concerns about Stumme's confusion about gemination and velarization, as well as his use of the "annexed" state as a syntactic device, seem almost minor in view of the nature and speed of Stumme's project.[5] The example Stroomer gives for gemination demonstrates how Stumme often did not know when to use it. Stroomer does not mention that the word in question, *khettab* (woodcutter), is actually a loanword from Arabic, where lack of attention to gemination could lead to an actual lack of meaning. Such words say much about the complexity of the stories Stumme collected. The Berber dialects of Morocco contain quite a few Arabic loanwords, and the transliterated tales show them in their "Berberized" forms. Stroomer's comments about Stumme's uncertain use of velarization stem in part from the same loanword problem. When one uses Roman script to write Arabic phonetically, properly placed diacritics aid comprehension.[6] Until students have significant spoken and written language skills, they necessarily depend on such visual markers. Problems of

[5] Stroomer points out that Hans Stumme often did not know when a consonant was geminated (doubled, indicating stress) or velarized (emphatic and pronounced with tongue and the upper palate). The difficulty seems readily apparent. Stumme would have written what he had heard, and if he did not hear things properly, or if he were not in the habit of writing Semitic languages in roman script, it is only natural that he would have confused consonants. Such aural refinement usually takes a bit to develop, and a total of five years of intermittent language study with someone else could have yielded nothing.

[6] Diacritics are marks that appear either above or below a letter to determine how the letter is pronounced. An example from French would be *français* (French), where the mark under the c, the cedilla, indicates a soft *"c"* (as in "nice") as opposed to a hard *"c"* (as in "catalog").

gemination and velarization are not as pressing when one is using Arabic script, as the letters in question appear in their normal form, thereby making evident how they should be pronounced.[7]

The last category in table 1, the "annexed" state (*l'état d'annexion*), refers to how words and word stems are linked. In his discussion of the Stumme work, Stroomer notes its uneven use. When one considers that Stumme would have written the stories as he heard them and remembers the quickness with which Stumme learned a variety of languages, it is surprising that one can make sense of anything. Stumme's transliterations use German phonetics, and in thinking about his uses of the "annexed" state, one can easily imagine his thinking in German, a language that uses compound words fairly regularly. The example given in table 1 is one of many. Stroomer gives the phrase sample *htigimenu* (at my house) as one example of Stumme's usage. Here, the now standard word for "in" or "at," *x,* is spelled with an *h* that is connected to the word for "house," *tigime,* according to Stroomer, *tigemmi* by others. The third element, *nu,* is the stem for the possessive of the first-person singular. While Stumme's spellings and affixed version are clearly incorrect, Stroomer's setting the word completely apart as he does in the table is not so common.[8] One is more likely to see something like *tigemmi-inu,* with the *nu* separated from the noun by a hyphen.[9] Though not exactly like German compound-word formation, Stumme's annexing might very well have followed a similar logic.

Stroomer's transliterative choices are not all clear either. For someone familiar with the language, his transliterations of the Tachelhit words are not as obvious as they could be. The difficulties start with the transliteration table that Stroomer erroneously refers to as the "transcription" table. He assigns linguistic terms to letters without giving explanations or sound

[7] Arabic diacritics simplify reading as they determine consonants and indicate vowels, thereby allowing one to pronounce a word even if one does not actually know the word.

[8] Orthographic rules for Tachelhit are still in the making. People in Morocco use both arabic and roman script to write in the Berber dialects. In France, researchers at the Institut National de Langues et Civilisations Orientales (INALCO) have begun standardizing spellings in roman alphabet based on French phonetics. They are the premier French center for such studies. Berber studies is a growing field. While I know little about Harry Stroomer's training, I suspect that, like me, he probably spent some time at INALCO in Paris or reading the Protectorate-era grammar books and dictionaries.

[9] This is an interesting point as the two *i*'s together suggest a long sound. How this should be transcribed is an interesting point. Stroomer's removing the second *i* might be just the thing.

equivalents that show how they are to be pronounced, that is, individual phonemes are given with no accompanying morpheme that shows their expression. At another level of phoneme and potential morpheme complication, Stroomer transliterates the word "dog" as *aydi* as opposed to *ayyidi,* the form used by the older French ethnographer and grammarian Robert Aspinion. While someone familiar with Tachelhit might sort out the pronunciation from memory, a beginning nonnative speaker of English might not. Anyone who has heard a small child go on about his dog in Tachelhit would probably more readily see how to pronounce it when spelled *ayyidi.*[10] Stroomer's use of the terms "high" and "low" to describe vowels is equally confusing for someone more accustomed to hearing or reading about long and short vowels. Again, with no explanation or words given to show what is meant by it all, the terms have very little meaning. As with the biographical sketch, this section was clearly done quickly and without much attention to detail.

Harry Stroomer actually translates the stories very well. The English reads smoothly and shows virtually no signs of language interference. In the story "The Girl Who Once Lived Among the Gazelles," Stroomer translates the word *imensi* as "meal" (as opposed to "dinner") and *luzir* as "vizier," but apart from that, no truly egregious translation mistakes jump to the eye.[11] When confusions do arise they have less to do with the English and more to do with the words used in the transliterated text. Stroomer is clearly comfortable with the original texts but, unlike the soldier-cum-ethnographer L. V. Justinard in the title of his *Poésies en dialecte du Sous marocain: D'après un manuscrit arabico-berbere,* does not indicate that Arabic words appear throughout the collection.[12] Different words might appear in the same text with the same meaning. In the story, one sees the word *imal* (Arabic: money) and the word *flus* (Arabic: money) in another. A similar switch occurs with the words *mlih* and *waxxa* (alternate spelling: *wa kha*), both translated as "all right." Again for someone

[10] During one of my visits to Tazerwalt, I learned that my host's son had "found" a dog. He seemed very happy about it and insisted on giving me the details of his find.

[11] One suspects that the confusing equivalence between *luzir* and "vizier" might stem from Stumme's having heard the word pronounced quickly. He would have heard the word *al-wazîr* and transliterated the *w* as *u.* Stroomer himself used the equally odd *v* for the English translation "vizier," which is more similar to a Farsi or Hindi speaker's use than to the actual Arabic word.

[12] L. V. Justinard, "Poésies en dialecte du Sous marocain: D'après un manuscrit arabico-berbère," *Journal asiatique* 213 (October–December 1928): 217–51.

familiar with the languages and the mixing that one can hear in the village, there is no problem. For the novice with little experience of either Arabic or Tachelhit, such switches might seem surprising when not completely confusing. Reading the English, however, one would never know.

Conclusion

As with all translation projects, Harry Stroomer's *Tashelhiyt Berber Folktales* has its problems. In addition to those normally faced by translators (meaning and context), Harry Stroomer has the added problem of transliterating a language that scholars are still attempting to standardize from a collection of texts already some one hundred years old. What Stroomer does under such conditions is consequently quite impressive. In spite of its flaws, Harry Stroomer's *Tashelhiyt Berber Folktales from Tazerwalt (South Morocco)* is a welcome addition to what one hopes is a growing body of English-language material on Berber culture and society.

MEDIATION AND THE PERFORMANCE OF RELIGIOUS AUTHORITY IN SENEGAL

Fiona Mc Laughlin and Babacar Mboup

Introduction

In her insightful study of the anthropology of African texts, Karin Barber states that with regard to language, "writing is not what confers textuality. Rather, what does is the quality of being joined together and given a recognisable existence as a form."[1] In this essay we are concerned with one of the myriad ways in which Wolof[2] discourse in Senegal is given such a recognizable existence and how the resultant form, namely that of verbal mediation, is deployed to enhance the religious and political authority of important Muslim shaykhs, known locally in French as marabouts, and in Wolof as *sériñ.* The form we explore is that of a discourse characterized by verbal mediation or surrogate speech whereby one person speaks as an intermediary on behalf of another.[3] In Wolof the "intermediary" is known as a *jottalikat,* a term that we will use throughout this essay. Mediated speech is not, in and of itself, an exceptional phenomenon since

[1] Karin Barber, *The Anthropology of Texts, Persons and Publics: Oral and Written Culture in Africa and Beyond* (Cambridge: Cambridge University Press, 2007), 1.

[2] Wolof is member of the Atlantic branch of the Niger-Congo family of languages, and is spoken primarily in Senegal, where it has become an urban vernacular and national lingua franca. It is also spoken to a lesser extent in Gambia and Mauritania.

[3] Kwesi Yankah, *Speaking for the Chief: Okyeame and the Politics of Akan Royal Oratory* (Bloomington: Indiana University Press, 1995).

Islamic Africa, VOL. 1, NO. 1, 2010. ISSN 2154-0993. www.islamicafricajournal.org

intermediaries exist in all societies and range from the American White House spokesman who speaks on behalf of the president to the Ghanaian *okyeame* who speaks on behalf of the Asante chief. What is remarkable about the specifically Sahelian form of surrogate speech, of which Wolof is but one example, is that both the figure of authority and the *jottalikat* are present and participate together in creating the discourse. The resultant form is a dyadic one characterized by a type of verbal echoing on the part of the *jottalikat* via the almost verbatim repetition of every phrase that the authority figure utters, as illustrated in the following short example that was taken from the text we propose to analyze in this essay:[4]

Marabout:	Gisal Muusa	Recall Moses
Jottalikat:	Gisal Muusa	Recall Moses
Marabout:	Ci suuf	Here below
Jottalikat:	Mu ne ci suuf	He said, here below
Marabout:	Dafa ne ko woon	He told him
Jottalikat:	Daf ne ko woon	He told him
Marabout:	Summil say dàll	Take off your shoes
Jottalikat:	Summil say dàll	Take off your shoes

From a purely functional point of view, the iteration of the phrase by the *jottalikat* can be superfluous. While it is often true that authoritative figures such as a marabout will render their speech difficult for the audience to understand by speaking quietly or mumbling, in many cases their speech is robust and comprehensible to the audience who in essence hear it twice. Clearly, something other than the mere transmission of a message is taking place. We argue in this essay that what is going on here is the creation of a text by which, following Barber, we mean a purposeful weaving together of words intended to attract attention and outlive the moment of its utterance—a text that will be repeated and circulated.[5] Furthermore, we propose that the dyadic nature of such a text does not simply reflect

---

[4] The text and its origin are discussed below in the section on Marabouts and Their Audiences. The original text is in Wolof, and the English translation is by the authors.

[5] Barber, *Anthropology of Texts.*

the authority of the marabout but is in fact constitutive of it. Our analysis draws most immediately from the work of Richard Bauman who proposes an insightful framework for understanding what is accomplished by mediated speech, and from Mc Laughlin and Villalón who present an analysis of the performance of a dyadic text between a Senegalese marabout and a *jottalikat* which is based on Bauman's work.[6] While the performance described by Mc Laughlin and Villalón takes place in a religious context, the text we analyze here is more overtly political in nature and involves the visit of an opposition candidate for the Senegalese presidency to the home of a prominent marabout, the caliph of the Tijaniyya Sufi order, in the city of Tivaouane.

Islam and the Institutionalization of a Religious Hierarchy

Senegal is a predominantly Muslim society where approximately 94 percent of the population adheres to Islam. Of these, the vast majority are Sufi Muslims for whom religious life is mediated through a spiritual guide who has access to esoteric religious knowledge and serves as an exemplar. Although there have been Muslims in what is now Senegal since the eleventh century, the bulk of the population embraced the religion during the latter half of the nineteenth and the first half of the twentieth centuries. The main Sufi orders to which the majority of the Senegalese population belong include the Tijaniyya, founded in nineteenth-century Algeria by Shaykh Ahmed al-Tijani; the Qadiriyya, founded by Abd el-Qadir al-Jilani in twelfth-century Baghdad; and two indigenous orders, the Mourides (sometimes Arabized as Muridiyya), founded by Amadou Bamba Mbacké (1850–1927), and the Layène order founded by Seydina Limamou Laye (1843–1909). Of these, the Tijaniyya has the greatest number of followers in Senegal, followed by the Mourides. The Tijaniyya has two main branches in Senegal, one founded by El Hajj Malick Sy (1855–1922) in the city of Tivaouane, and the other—founded by Abdoulaye Niasse (c.1845–1922)—based in the city of Kaolack. The orders differ from each

[6] Richard Bauman, *A World of Others' Words* (Malden, Mass.: Blackwell, 2004); Fiona Mc Laughlin and Leonardo A. Villalón, "Mettre en scène la légitimité: Un discours de feu Xalifa Abdoul Aziz Sy et de son *jottalikat,*" in *Communication et société Wolof: Héritage et création,* ed. Anna Diagne, Sascha Kesseler, and Christian Meyer, 303–27 (Paris: L'Harmattan, 2010).

other in a variety of ways that include their understanding of the nature of the marabout-disciple relationship, the relative emphasis placed on various activities such as prayer and work, the nature of the initiation rites and prayer sequences, as well as numerous other factors, but all can be said to follow the general practices more broadly associated with Sufism. Although Sufism is certainly not uncontested in Senegal, it remains the dominant mode of Islamic practice in the country.

Colonial officials and scholars alike have long been fascinated by the unique and distinctive social manifestations of Senegalese Sufism that, far more than anywhere else in the region, is characterized by a high degree of formalization and institutionalization. Building on the local association of disciples known as the *daaira,* the orders have gradually developed a highly structured set of relationships that reach out from the religious centers (zawiyas) and today include networks of associations spanning the diaspora across the globe.[7] At work are a complex set of factors that include personal charisma, political alliances, lineages and genealogies, and increasingly global economic networks. This high degree of organization has made the Sufi orders, and the major marabouts, actors with extraordinary weight in Senegalese social, political, and economic life.

From early on in the colonial period the French recognized the potential significance of these organized social structures centered on charismatic marabouts, and what began as a conflictual relationship between colonial and religious authorities eventually gave way to what David Robinson, in his eponymous book, has termed "paths of accommodation," namely a symbiotic relationship of sorts between the two.[8] These paths of accommodation, begun in the colonial period, have done much to shape the Senegalese religio-political landscape. Senegal's first president,

[7] Cheikh Anta Babou, "Brotherhood Solidarity, Education and Migration: The Role of the Dahiras Among the Murid Muslim Community of New York," *African Affairs* 101 (2002): 151–70; Beth Anne Buggenhagen, "Beyond Brotherhood: Gender, Religious Authority, and the Global Circuits of Senegalese Muridiyya," in *New Perspectives on Islam in Senegal: Conversion, Migration, Wealth, Power and Femininity,* ed. Mamadou Diouf and Mara A. Leichtman,189–210 (New York: Palgrave, 2008); Leonardo A. Villalón, "Sufi Modernities in Contemporary Senegal: Religious Dynamics Between the Local and the Global," in *Sufism and the Modern in Islam,* ed. Martin van Bruinessen and Julia Day Howell, 172–91 (London: I. B. Tauris, 2007).

[8] David Robinson, *Paths of Accommodation: Muslim Societies and French Colonial Authorities in Senegal and Mauritania,1880–1920* (Athens: Ohio University Press, 2000).

Léopold Sédar Senghor, as well as his successor, Abdou Diouf, both cognizant of the political power of religious leaders, cultivated good relations with marabouts, and the close relationship between the state and religious authorities became a defining aspect of postindependence politics in Senegal.[9]

Both the spiritual authority of the Sufi orders and the nature of their relationship to the state have not gone uncontested, however. Long-standing contestation by reformist groups such as the Jama'at Ibadu Rahman has been joined in recent years by a multiplicity of voices from both outside the Sufi system and also from within it, as generational shifts in power open up the terrain for competition between the sons and grandsons of the charismatic founders, Amadou Bamba Mbacké on the part of the Mourides and El Hajj Malick Sy in the case of the Tivaouane branch of the Tijaniyya.[10] Since Abdoulaye Wade, a perennial opposition candidate, assumed the presidency in 2000 and immediately demonstrated a pro-Mouride position from which he then had to distance himself, the relationship between the state and religious authorities has become increasingly complex and fragmented. There is no longer anything monolithic about this relationship, and although the marabouts in general maintain a strong presence on the political scene, they are cultivated not only by those in power but also by opposition leaders and are subject to a fluid and polyvalent set of discourses that critique their various roles, both spiritual and political. It is against this backdrop, where the relationship between marabouts and the state is continuously negotiated, that the performance of religious authority that we seek to analyze takes place.

---

[9] Donal B. Cruise O'Brien, *The Mourides of Senegal: The Political and Economic Organisation of an Islamic Brotherhood* (Oxford: Clarendon Press, 1971); Donal B. Cruise O'Brien, *Saints and Politicians: Essays in the Organisation of a Senegalese Peasant Society* (Cambridge: Cambridge University Press, 1975); Donal B. Cruise O'Brien, *Symbolic Confrontations: Muslims Imagining the State in Africa* (New York: Palgrave, 2003); Jean Copans, *Les marabouts de l'arachide: La confrèrie mouride et les paysans du Sénégal* (Paris: Le Sycomore, 1980); Christian Coulon, *Le marabout et le prince: Islam et pouvoir au Sénégal* (Paris: Pedone), 1981; Leonardo A. Villalón, "Sufi Rituals as Rallies: Religious Ceremonies in the Politics of Senegalese State-Society Relations," *Comparative Politics* 26 (1994): 4; Leonardo A. Villalón, "Islamic Society and State Power in Senegal: Disciples and Citizens in Fatick" (Cambridge: Cambridge University Press, 1995).

[10] Leonardo A. Villalón, "Generational Changes, Political Stagnation, and the Evolving Dynamics of Religion and Politics in Senegal" *Africa Today* 46, nos. 3–4 (1999): 129–47.

Mediation in Wolof Oral Culture

Mediated speech, whereby a message originating with a person of authority or high social status is transmitted to an audience via the intermediary of a verbal specialist, is one of the primary means of enacting authority in many West African societies. In the Asante courts of Ghana, for example, the *okyeame* serves as a spokesman for the *asentehene* (king), and in the Mande world and other societies of the Western Sahel the *jali* (griot) serves as an intermediary for notables and their publics.[11] Mediated or surrogate speech has long been noted in discussions of West African verbal art, but few studies have been devoted to more than a superficial analysis of the phenomenon,[12] tending rather to focus on the tangential although equally interesting question of the social role of the mediator, especially as it relates to questions of differentiation and status. Wolof society, like most societies of the western Sahel, is highly stratified and hierarchical and includes groups known as *géer,* a term that is often translated as "nobles," as well as several endogamous "artisan" groups, known as "*ñeeño*" in Wolof, whose power derives from specialized knowledge and techniques associated with dangerous or volatile substances.[13] These include, among others, *tëgg* (blacksmiths), *uude* (leatherworkers), and *géwël* (griots). *Tëgg* work with fire and the transformation of metal, and *uude* work with the blood and skins of animals. The power of the *géwël* derives from their ability to work with the "substance" of words.

The social differentiation of these groups, which is often accompanied by stigmatization, as well as their practice of endogamy, has led anthropologists to consider them in light of other caste systems found in societies throughout the world. One of the outcomes of the inclusion of Sahelian groups in this comparison is a general rethinking of the notion of caste as a useful construct, as evidenced by the rich and varied scholarship that has recently emerged on the topic. While some scholars (such as Tal Tamari, Barbara G. Hoffman, and Roy M. Dilley) maintain the terminology while

---

[11] Yankah, *Speaking for the Chief.*

[12] Notable exceptions include Yankah's 1995 study of *akyeame* (singular: *okyeame*), orators in the Akan royal courts (see Yankah, *Speaking for the Chief*), and Irvine's 1996 work on the indeterminacy of participant roles in mediation (see Judith T. Irvine, "Shadow Conversations: The Indeterminacy of Participant Roles," in *Natural Histories of Discourse,* ed. Michael Silverstein and Greg Urban [Chicago: University of Chicago Press, 1996]).

[13] Abdoulaye-Bara Diop, *La société wolof, tradition et changement: Les systèmes d'inégalité et de domination* (Paris: Karthala, 1981).

redefining to a certain extent what it means, others (such as Bonnie L. Wright, David C. Conrad and Barbara E. Frank, Jan Jansen, and Marloes Janson), tend to eschew the term "caste" as they propose new and interesting ways of conceptualizing the phenomenon.[14]

In Wolof oral culture the norms of mediated speech are largely negotiated by *géwël.* Originally attached to noble families, they perform a variety of functions including praise singing, the recitation of genealogy and family histories, and verbal mediation. While these functions are still carried out at major life events such as naming ceremonies and marriages, *géwël* have also adapted their art to changing circumstances within Senegalese society over the centuries.[15] Muezzins in Senegal, for example, are frequently of *géwël* origin, and they also play important roles in radio, television, and advertising, as well as in more traditional sectors. If higher government officials who make public national addresses do not normally employ the services of a *géwël* because they view it as a folkloric display at odds with the modern image they seek to project, at a more local level their addresses are often mediated by *géwël,* especially when they are incorporated into larger public ceremonies. Marabouts, on the other hand, typically take full advantage of such resources and employ griots to good effect in order to enhance their authority and legitimacy.

Just as the roles of contemporary *géwël* have adapted to changing circumstances in Senegalese life, so too has the role of mediator been assumed by others who are not, by heritage, *géwël. Géwël* constitute a social group that often assumes the role of *jottalikat* or mediator, but non-*géwël* can also fulfill that role. It is interesting to note, however, that non-*géwël* who assume the role of *jottalikat* also generally assume the speech

---

[14] Tal Tamari, *Les castes de l'Afrique occidentale: Artisans et musiciens endogames* (Nanterre: Société d'ethnologie, 1997); Barbara G. Hoffman, *Griots at War: Conflict, Conciliation, and Caste in Mande* (Bloomington: Indiana University Press, 2000); Roy M. Dilley, *Islamic and Caste Knowledge Practices Among Haalpulaar'en in Senegal* (Edinburgh: Edinburgh University Press, 2004); Bonnie L. Wright, "The Power of Articulation," in *Creativity of Power: Cosmology and Action in African Societies,* ed. W. Arens and I. Karp (Washington, D.C.: Smithsonian Institution Press, 1989); David C. Conrad and Barbara E. Frank, eds., *Status and Identity in West Africa: Nyamakalaw of Mande* (Bloomington: Indiana University Press, 1995); Jan Jansen, *The Griot's Craft* (Münster: Lit Verlag, 2000); Marloes Janson, *The Best Hand Is the Hand That Always Gives: Griottes and Their Profession in Eastern Gambia* (Leiden: CNWS Publications, 2002).

[15] For a discussion of some of these modern adaptations, see Cornelia Panzacchi, "The Livelihoods of Traditional Griots in Modern Senegal," *Africa* 64, no. 2 (1994): 190–210.

characteristics of *géwël,* thereby implicitly acknowledging the fact that the norms of public discourse have been established by the latter.

Marabouts and Their Audiences

Of the many Sufi rituals and pilgrimages that punctuate the Senegalese Islamic calendar, all bring together large numbers of disciples to celebrate and reinforce the most central relationship of Senegalese religious organization, namely that between a marabout and his disciples, or *taalibe* as they are known in Wolof. Drawing on a history that dates from the colonial period, a set of structured forms and patterns for such events has emerged to form a coherent, and uniquely Senegalese, cultural repertoire of symbols and rituals that serve to fulfill their core purpose, which is the legitimation of authority among marabouts. During such events key messages are transmitted to various audiences through the enactment of ritual activities that are charged with cultural meaning. The symbolic rituals have evolved to have a uniquely Senegalese meaning, and they draw on myriad historical factors that have shaped contemporary Senegalese culture. These include elements of what Thomas A. Hale and Paul Stoller have called, albeit ahistorically, a "deep Sahelian culture," with its entrenched notions of social hierarchy and stratification as well as the centrality of generosity and redistribution in maintaining social standing.[16] Upon this has been built a strongly Muslim culture which draws on the rich heritage of Sufism with its core characteristics of mystical knowledge and emphasis on the role of a spiritual guide. The social organization of Sufism in Senegal has also been heavily shaped by the elaboration of colonial and postcolonial state structures, as discussed by Leonardo A. Villalón.[17] Taken as a whole, these elements that draw from various traditions and incorporate multiple innovations constitute the core of what might be termed a unique Senegalese Sufi culture.

Senegalese Sufi ceremonies are multifaceted rituals that often have multiple messages and multiple audiences. The central audience is always made up of members of the religious community, namely the *taalibes,* or "disciples," of the particular marabout or lineage to whom the ceremony

---

[16] Thomas A. Hale and Paul Stoller, "Oral Art, Society, and Survival in the Sahel Zone," in *African Literature Studies: The Present State/l'état Present,* ed. Stephen Arnold, 163–69 (Washington, D.C.: Three Continents Press, African Literature Association, and Institute for Research in Comparative Literature, 1985).

[17] Villalón, "Sufi Rituals."

is dedicated. The message in such cases emphasizes the centrality of the role of the Sufi guide, and at a more immediate level the message concerns the attributes and charisma of the specific marabout or lineage in question, thereby showing that they merit the loyalty and devotion of their followers. External audiences may include other, occasionally rival, religious communities, but the primary external audience is the Senegalese state. Through public demonstrations of size and fervor of a marabout's following, and hence political power, these religious ceremonies communicate to the state the importance of the marabouts and the necessity of taking them into account in the elaboration of public policies. In recognition of this fact, the state often sends it representatives to these ceremonies where marabouts are accorded a place of honor.

Messages to both internal and external audiences, namely the religious community and the state, are transmitted in multiple ways, both verbal and symbolic. As Irvine has noted in her work on Wolof discourse, verbal messages are often, and perhaps most effectively, communicated indirectly via stories and parables, as well as Hadiths in the Islamic tradition, that then require further discussion to access their deeper meanings.[18] The story itself is thus posed as an object for discussion, and in the process of discussion the core messages are transmitted. Through all these means, religious events serve primarily to enact and communicate the legitimacy, both religious and sociopolitical, of the religious leader. This symbolic legitimation of authority of the marabout in the eyes of both disciples and the state is enhanced, as we shall see, by the mediated verbal performance of both marabout and *jottalikat.*

The Performance

The speech event that we take here to illustrate the performance of maraboutic authority took place in Tivaouane in March of 2009 on the eve of the Mawlud, or celebration of the birthday of the Prophet. Known in Wolof as the *gàmmu,* this holiday is one of the most important in the Muslim calendar, and it has taken on a special significance for the Tivaouane branch of the Tijaniyya in Senegal. It is celebrated by a nocturnal ceremony during which praise poems are chanted and sung to the Prophet Muhammad; to El Hajj Malik Sy, founder of the zawiya; and to his son and successor to

[18] Judith T. Irvine, "Communication et société wolof à travers le temps et l'espace," in *Communication et société wolof: Héritage et création,* ed. Anna Diagne, Sascha Kesseler, and Christian Meyer (Paris: L'Harmattan, 2010).

the caliphate, Ababacar Sy, who died in 1957. The *gàmmu* has also been the site of rivalries between competing marabouts from the Sy family who often have their own praise songs added to the illustrious litany.[19]

The speech event takes place during a visit by Idrissa Seck, a prominent and controversial politician, to the current caliph of the Tivaouane branch of the Tijaniyya, Sëriñ Mansour Sy. [20] The meeting was of great interest to the Senegalese public and was covered extensively in the Senegalese press, recorded and broadcast, and posted on the Internet, thereby exponentially increasing the audience. Erstwhile protégé of President Abdoulaye Wade, Seck served as prime minister of Senegal under Wade from 2002–2004. He then formed his own opposition party, Rewmi, in 2006 and ran against Wade, unsuccessfully, for president in 2007. Since then, Seck and Wade appear at times to have reconciled their differences, but Seck, who is currently mayor of the city of Thiès, continues to position himself for a future run for the presidency. Maraboutic support, which he received from Sëriñ Mansour Sy at the time of the speech, would be an important asset in his eventual candidacy for the presidency. Seck was received at the marabout's home in Tivaouane in relatively opulent surroundings, in the presence of various notables dressed in their finest garments. The mirrored room where the speech takes place was crowded with Sériñ Mansour Sy's retinue, Idrissa Seck, and with the most prominent members of his Rewmi political party, two or three *géwël,* and some learned disciples of the marabout. When the marabout entered the room he greeted various people in the audience and joked with them before taking a seat on an ornate sofa next to the chair in which Seck was sitting. Most notable among the marabout's retinue was Habib Sy, his son and a potential successor to the caliphate. In what appears to be a carefully orchestrated display of authority, Habib Sy is called up to the front to serve as *jottalikat,* an exceptional role for a person of his stature, but one that gives him great visibility in front of Idrissa Seck, himself a potential successor to the Senegalese presidency. Here, the politics of potentiality play out as the multiple audiences are invited to envisage a possible future in which Idrissa Seck is president of the republic, and Habib Sy caliph of the Tivaouane Tijaniyya.

[19] Fiona Mc Laughlin, "'In the Name of God I Will Sing Again, Mawdo Malik the Good': Popular Music and the Senegalese Sufi *Tariqas,*" *Journal of Religion in Africa* 30, no. 2 (2000): 191–207, 194.

[20] A video recording of the speech can be viewed at the following website, an unstable URL: http://xibar.net/VIDEO-PHOTOS-VISITE-DE-IDRISSA-SECK-A-TIVAOUANE _a15281.html (downloaded in August and September, 2009).

Habib Sy first mediates for Idrissa Seck who, as the visitor, conveys his greetings to the marabout, Sériñ Mansour Sy. When those greetings are finished, Habib Sy then serves as *jottalikat* for his father, the marabout, for most of his speech, but two griots are also involved in the event as singers and reciters, and one of them takes over the role of *jottalikat* towards the latter part of the speech.

The structure of the speech revolves around several stories or parables drawn from the Qur'an and the Hadiths concerning God, the Prophet Muhammad, and Moses, which contain numerous paradoxes. References to his lineage serve to legitimate Sériñ Mansour Sy's standing as a patriarch and holy man since he is the grandson of El Hajj Malik Sy (1855–1922), the founder of the Senegalese Tijaniyya; the son of Ababacar Sy (1885–1957), the second caliph of the Tivaouane branch of the Tijaniyya; and the nephew of Abdou Aziz Sy (1904–1997), whom he succeeded as caliph. Large portraits of these men are positioned prominently in the house, thus providing a visual reminder of the genealogy which is reinforced by the verbal one. After formally greeting Idrissa Seck, the marabout evokes his illustrious forebears by recounting what Baay (his father, Ababacar) used to say when receiving guests, then invoking his grandfather, El Hajj Malik. The fact that Sériñ Mansour Sy's son, Habib Sy, is the *jottalikat* for most of this speech serves to enhance the notion of holy lineage because four generations are thus represented in the event, from El Hajj Malik, the founder, by evocation, to his great-grandson, Habib, who is present.

Habib Sy's role in the verbal performance is that of *jottalikat,* a Wolof word meaning "one who transmits," which comes from the verb *jottali,* "to transmit or pass," and the agent suffix *-kat,* which is the equivalent of the English agent suffix *–er,* as in the words "singer" and "writer." His role is first and foremost to replicate his father's utterances, which he does for the most part verbatim. The role of the marabout, who participates as the originator of the message, by contrast, is that of "source," and the audience has the role of "target." Following Bauman, we will refer to the Marabout's speech as the "source dialogue," composed of source utterances, and to the *jottalikat*'s speech as the "target dialogue," likewise composed of target utterances.[21] Verbal mediation of this sort sets up an indexical relationship between the source dialogue and the target dialogue where each

[21] Bauman, *World of Others' Words,* 133. The theoretical arguments we make here are similar to those made in Mc Laughlin and Villalón with regard to a 1994 maraboutic address by Abdou Aziz Sy, Sériñ Mansour Sy's immediate predecessor as caliph. See further Mc Laughlin and Villalón, "Mettre en scène."

part is structured by its relation to the other.[22] The source utterance reaches ahead to the target utterance by anticipating it, and the latter reaches back to the source by replicating it in such a way that "the routine cannot be dissolved into two independent dyads" since each part is structured by its relation to the other.[23]

In mediational performances the target utterance is understood by the audience to be a replication of some source utterance, and in this particular instance the *jottalikat* is replicating the marabout's utterance. Urban, in a groundbreaking essay on replication, states that replication "is an attempt at reproduction, at relocating the original instance of discourse to a new context—carrying something over from the earlier to the later one."[24] Following Urban, Bauman takes the term "replication" to mean "the reproduction of an instance of discourse in a new context, in a relationship of copy to original."[25] Although the replication is temporally juxtaposed with the original, it is nevertheless in a new context since it is being uttered by a second participant, the *jottalikat,* and it has entered into the linguistic context as an utterance subsequent to a prior version. As Bauman shows, many, if not most, mediators conventionally transfer the message exactly as it was uttered by the source, so that the source message is transferred verbatim and intact. While this is often the case with Wolof mediators or *jottalikat,* there is also sometimes room for what Bauman calls "infiltration" of the source text by the mediator, who changes or embellishes the original through the use of synonyms, alternative syntactic structures, code switching, or a variety of other devices that add an aesthetic dimension to the target message, and which are uniquely the domain of the *jottalikat* and constitute the essence of his verbal artistry and skill.

Bauman claims that three things are being accomplished through mediational performance, namely, "traditionalization," "socialization of knowledge," and "authorization," all of which are highly interrelated. "Traditionalization" is defined as the process by which something, in this case discourse, becomes part of tradition by enduring beyond its initial

---

22 Judith T. Irvine, "Shadow Conversations: The Indeterminacy of Participant Roles," in *Natural Histories of Discourse,* ed. Michael Silverstein and Greg Urban (Chicago: University of Chicago Press, 1996); Bauman, *World of Others' Words.*

23 Bauman, *World of Other's Words,* 130.

24 Greg Urban. "Entextualization, Replication, and Power," in *Natural histories of Discourse,* ed. Michael Silverstein and Greg Urban, 21–44, 21 (Chicago: University of Chicago Press, 1996).

25 Bauman, *World of Others' Words,* 129.

instantiation, thereby transcending time. Traditionalization is furthermore accomplished through the "active creation of a connection linking current discourse to past discourse."[26] Viewed from this perspective, the replication and recontextualization of the source discourse by the *jottalikat* literally enacts the nuclear structure of traditionalization since the source message extends beyond its initial instantiation in being replicated by the *jottalikat* as a target message. For Bauman, mediational routines such as the one under discussion here constitute a formalized and routinized way of accomplishing what is minimally necessary for traditionalization to take place.

This perspective leads us back to the participants in the mediational performance in order to examine how they structure their participation so as to contribute to the enactment of "traditionalization." The three major participants, all of whom are minimally necessary to the enactment, are the source of the utterance (here the Marabout, Sériñ Mansour Sy), the mediator who replicates the message in a new context (the *jottalikat,* Habib Sy, and later the *géwël*), and the audience, which includes most immediately Idrissa Seck, his entourage, and the marabout's entourage but which goes out to a much wider audience, thanks to the use of electronic media. With regard to the marabout and the *jottalikat,* as stated above, there is an indexical relationship between the source dialogue and the target dialogue such that the former anticipates the latter, and the latter is predicated on the former, so that the inextricability of the two is once again underscored. The enactment of traditionalization must, by definition, be a public enactment. The audience is thus a necessary component of the mediational performance which could not take place without them. As this speech was so widely covered in the media, and given the fact that it is still available for viewing on the Internet, the audience went well beyond the immediate, physically present audience in both space and time.

The second accomplishment of the type of routinized mediation described in this essay is the "socialization of knowledge," by which is meant the enactment "and display in elementary form of the social currency of texts, their dissemination beyond a single individual source and their incorporation into the stock of usable knowledge available to others."[27] The means by which this is accomplished involves all three participant roles in the performance: that of the marabout, the *jottalikat,* and the audience.

[26] Ibid., 147.
[27] Ibid., 149.

We have already seen how the marabout and *jottalikat* work in tandem to enact the nuclear structure of traditionalization. The socialization of the knowledge that originates with Sériñ Mansour Sy is accomplished through its transmittal to an audience of many people, namely to society, by Habib Sy. The process of socialization of knowledge can then be passed on to other individuals and audiences, as is the case with the performance under discussion, since it was videotaped and broadcast on television and the Internet for even further dissemination or socialization. Mediational performance is public performance—thus the socialization of transmitted knowledge is assured.

In addition to the enactment of traditionalization and the socialization of knowledge, the mediational performance also enacts the core process of authorization in rendering a discourse authoritative. Bauman invokes Bakhtin's conception of authoritative discourse as having "its authority already fused to it. . . . Its authority was already acknowledged in the past. It is a prior discourse" but points out that Bakhtin fails to consider *how* discourse becomes authoritative, considering it simply as a fait accompli.[28] The enactment of authorization via mediational performance is linked to the two processes discussed above. Traditionalization establishes it, literally, as a prior discourse through replication, and the transmittal of the discourse to a larger audience is responsible for the socialization of knowledge contained within the discourse. Although both of these functions imply an authoritative source, the mediational performance also accomplishes authorization in a variety of ways. First, with regard to the participants, the source is generally of a higher social or political status than the mediator who relays the message. In the Wolof case, the *jottalikat* is often a *géwël* (griot) who is perceived to be of lower social status although his talents as an orator are highly valued. In the case of the speech under analysis, the marabout's son would automatically be seen as having lower status than his father: he is younger, and he is not the caliph. Second, the mediator's discourse is often subordinated to that of the source when the latter is transmitted verbatim. Although that is the case in the speech under discussion, it is not always true for Wolof mediated speech, as can be seen in other maraboutic discourses.[29]

Considering the possibility that the authoritativeness of a source

[28] See Mikhail M Bakhtin, *The Dialogic Imagination,* ed. Michael Holquist (Austin: University of Texas Press, 1981), 342. Bakhtin is cited in Bauman, *World of Others' Words,* 151.
[29] Mc Laughlin & Villalón, "Mettre en scène."

discourse emanates simply from the authority of the utterer, Bauman explores what the mediational performance adds and proposes that it "*enact(s)* the authorization of discourse, by making its authority manifest, objectifying it in overtly perceptible ways," adding that "(a)gency resides with the author; the mediator is denied an active role in the formulation and entextualization of the message. Rather he is bound by it."[30] But as Bauman recognizes, this latter statement is not accurate in all cases, including the Asante *okyeame* and the Wolof *jottalikat,* since in both cases there can be significant infiltration of the source utterance by the mediator. This type of infiltration, however, has its bounds. Although the words might be changed, added to, or embellished, they are nonetheless considered to be faithful to the original because they convey the same message even if they are reformulations rather than replicas.

Replication and Innovation

The dyadic nature of the discourse described above is the central aspect of the mediated performance, and neither the Marabout's speech nor that of the *jottalikat* can be extricated from each other in any meaningful way. But the space that can be opened up by reformulation rather than verbatim replication of Sériñ Mansour Sy's words points to a second type of authority enacted within the performance, namely the authority of the *jottalikat,* and in particular the *géwël* who intervene towards the end of the marabout's speech. Let us first consider the dyadic nature of the text as illustrated in the following excerpt concerning the notion of *sutura* which has the meaning of "discretion," a highly valued quality in Wolof society. Here, the marabout recounts a conversation he had with his father, El Hajj Malik, about *sutura,* which the latter describes with the word *rafet* (Wolof: beautiful; used in both a visual and moral sense). Habib Sy is the *jottalikat.*

Excerpt 1

Marabout:	Ma ne ko waaw Pàppa, sutura nu muy rafete? I said to him, So Papa, how can discretion be beautiful?	1
Jottalikat:	Mu ne ko waaw Pàppa, sutura nu muy rafete? He said to him, So Papa, how can discretion be beautiful?	2

[30] Bauman, *World of Other's Words,* 152.

Marabout: Nu muy ñaawe? 3
How can it be ugly?

Jottalikat: Nu muy ñaawe? 4
How can it be ugly?

Marabout: Mu ne ma, benn mbubb 5
He said to me, a gown

Jottalikat: Nee mu ne ko, benn mbubb 6
He said he said to him, a gown

Marabout: Nga sol yóbbu i tool. 7
You wear it to go to the fields.

Jottalikat: Nga sol yóbbu i tool 8
You wear it to go to the fields.

Marabout: Sol yóbbu i xew 9
You wear it to go to ceremonies

Jottalikat: Sol yóbbu i xew 10
You wear it to go to ceremonies

Marabout: Di ko fanaane 11
Wear it to sleep at night
Jottalikat: Di ko fanaane 12
Wear it to sleep at night

Marabout: Sutura la 13
It's discreet

Jottalikat: Sutura la 14
It's discreet

Marabout: Waaye rafetul 15
But it's not beautiful

Jottalikat: Waaye rafetul nag 16
But it's not beautiful at all

Marabout: Ma ne ko waaw! 17
I said to him, yes!

Jottalikat: Mu ne ko waaw! 18
He said to him, yes!

In this excerpt, which is quite typical of Habib's performance as *jottalikat,* the replication mirrors the original with almost no change other than what is entailed deictically by the switch in narrators, as in line 1 (Ma ne ko . . . [I said to him . . .]) and line 2 (Mu ne ko . . . [He said to him . . .]) and in line 17 (Ma ne ko waaw! [I said to him, "yes"!]) and line 18 (Mu ne ko waaw! [He said to him, "yes"!]). The only place that we hear Habib Sy's additional contribution to the discourse is in the emphasis he adds in line 16 and in the embellishment of the genealogy at the beginning of the speech where he even changes the referent of the marabout's speech. In the following excerpt the marabout, Sëriñ Mansour Sy, is referring to his father, Ababacar Sy, as Baay (father) in line 1, but Habib Sy switches the referent to Sériñ Mansour Sy's grandfather, El Hajj Malik Sy, in line 2. The marabout responds by changing his referent to Maam (grandfather) for several utterances, beginning in line 3, before switching back to talking about his father:

Excerpt 2

Marabout:	Baay, daaira bu mos a ñew ci moom Father, every time a *daaira*[31] came to him	1
Jottalikat:	Nee daaira bu mos a ñew ci Maam Seydi Ass Malik He said, every time a *daaira* came to Grandfather Seydi El Hajj Malik	2
Marabout:	Maam da daan a wax ne, seen tank yii yàlla na ko Yàlla def tanki yërmande Grandfather used to say, may God make your steps steps of compassion	3
Jottalikat:	Nee Maam dafa daan a wax ne seen tank yii yàlla na ko Yàlla def tanki yërmande He said, Grandfather used to say, may God make your steps steps of compassion	4

Whether this was a slip on the part of one of the participants or a conscious decision to switch the referent, the overall effect nonetheless emphasizes

[31] A *daaira* is a central institution of Senegalese Sufism. It consists of a close association of disciples of the same marabout or Sufi order, which forms the basis of everyday religious associational life and entails economic and social obligations and benefits.

the nested patriarchal structures and illustrious spiritual genealogy of the Sy family and magnifies and legitimates both Sériñ Mansour Sy and Habib Sy in the eyes of the audience.

Because of his status as *géer* (noble) as opposed to *ñeeño* (artisan), there are certain aspects of verbal mediation typically associated with *géwël* that are closed to Habib Sy and which are consequently handed over to the *géwël* (griots) who participate in the performance. The founder of the Tivaouane zawiya, El Hajj Malik Sy, was a prolific composer of praise poetry to the Prophet Muhammad, and the family and their disciples preserve his works by memorizing and reciting them on occasions such as the *gàmmu.* The Sy family *géwël* are especially conversant with El Hajj Malik's oeuvre and not only serve as a repository for them but can also turn them into songs at the request of the marabout. Although it is acceptable for Habib Sy to serve as a *jottalikat,* it would be unseemly for him to sing alone since he is not a *géwël;* thus, at the appropriate moment the marabout calls on the two *géwël* who participate in the speech event.

The presence of the *géwël* and their delivery of the marabout's words, along with their singing, create an atmosphere of ritual and importance in a ceremony that is both serious and lighthearted. Towards the latter part of his speech Sériñ Mansour Sy begins to recount a long story that culminates in a miracle performed by the Prophet Muhammad and decides to provide his grandfather El Hajj Malik's commentary on it. He invites the first *géwël,* seated to his left and wearing an outfit of bold striped cloth that contrasts with the damask gowns that virtually all the other men in the room are wearing, to sing one of El Hajj Malik's poems. But when the *géwël* stands up and starts singing, Sériñ Mansour stops him because it is evidently not the poem he wants. The marabout clarifies the context of the poem he wants, and the *géwël* starts to sing another poem which also turns out to be wrong. As the marabout is saying "No, no!" a second *géwël* comes out of the audience towards the front singing the right song, to which the marabout responds *Waaw kañ!* (Exactly!). The second *géwël* is ushered to the front and stands behind Idrissa Seck and Sériñ Mansour Sy, facing the audience. The first *géwël* is told by the marabout to sit back down. At this point Habib Sy resumes his transmission of the marabout's speech which is punctuated at various points by the singing of the second *géwël.* Sériñ Mansour Sy eventually arrives at the climax of the story: with a gesture of his hand, the Prophet Muhammad stops a stone in midair where it remains until today, at which point the first griot manages to reclaim his authority by singing an appropriate song and then taking over from Habib Sy as *jottalikat* for the remainder of the marabout's speech.

The *géwël*'s replication, like Habib Sy's, is a more or less verbatim copy of the marabout's speech, but the marabout also values the *géwël* for his ability to sing. At a certain point the marabout begins a poem in Arabic, which is also a way of legitimating his standing as a scholar of Islam. The *géwël* replicates the first lines of the poem but is interrupted by the marabout, who says, "I didn't say to recite it, I said to sing it." The *géwël* complies, and the marabout expresses his approval again with *Waaw kañ!* (Exactly!). Immediately following this, the marabout wants the *géwël* to recite a certain verse from the Qur'an, and there is some discussion as to which is the right one. After it is negotiated between the marabout in an everyday type of delivery, the *géwël* abruptly switches into his recitation style which is louder, higher pitched, and faster than normal speech. As the speech comes to a climax and Sériñ Mansour Sy cleverly poses a question that entails, as an answer, the political support of Idrissa Seck and his party, Rewmi, the *géwël* slightly embellishes the marabout's question. The second *géwël* then asks the question of Idrissa Seck, addressing him simply as "you," and the first *géwël* then asks Idrissa Seck to speak. The marabout then takes control of the situation and wraps up the speech by saying that the audience will not hear from him again on the matter until Idrissa Seck returns the following year.

Excerpt 3

Marabout:	Pourquoi? Why?	1
Géwël 1:	Pourquoi loolu? Why that?	2
Géwël 2:	Yaw lañ ko laaj We're asking you (the question)	3
Géwël 1:	Alaaji Idrissa waxal! El Hajj Idrissa, speak!	4
Marabout:	Bu ngeen ko ñamatee You won't hear of this again	5
Géwël 1:	Bu ngeen ko ñamatee You won't hear of this again	6

Marabout:	Idrissa dafa delusi déwén Until Idrissa comes back next year	7
Géwël 1:	Idrissa dafa delusi déwén. Until Idrissa comes back next year.	8

The room immediately bursts into noise as people start talking and exclaiming, and Sériñ Mansour Sy and Idrissa Seck get up to signal that the event is over.

This speech by Sériñ Mansour Sy was an important event in the dance that goes on between religious and political powers in Senegal. Idrissa Seck had come to Tivaouane as a disciple, but also to ask for the marabout's political support, which he got. The marabout was sought out for his support, and his political power was very much in evidence. The three accomplishments of the mediated speech event—namely traditionalization, socialization of knowledge, and authorization, which were enacted by Habib Sy and the two *géwël*—magnified the importance of the event, and magnified the marabout's authority and legitimacy with regard to both his disciples and the state.

Conclusion

We return now to the idea of a text with which we began this essay. In addition to the immediate interest of the political and religious contingencies of the context in which this speech was performed, what emerges as one of the most salient aspects of our discussion is the close relationship between texts and authority. Texts are created and set off from ordinary speech by being worked into a recognizable form, which in this case is the dyadic discourse created by a marabout and a mediator. This does not mean, however, that they are self-contained; on the contrary, they evoke in a fluid way other texts and other discourses. Witness Barber's encounter with *oríkì,* a genre of Yoruba praise poetry: "Every phrase led out to hinterlands of explanation. Every component of the shapeless, baggy text opened up into other narratives, other formulations, quotations from other texts. The text appeared to have no centre and no boundaries." "Subsequent study," she continues, "showed me that praise poetry genres across Africa work in a similar fashion—with differences."[32] The differences in the case of

[32] Barber, *Anthropology of Texts,* viii.

the type of mediated performances between marabout and *jottalikat* described in this essay lie in their relationship to other Islamic texts, such as the Qur'an and the Hadiths or sayings about the Prophet Muhammad, and to the local repertoire of Islamic texts about the exemplary qualities and miracles of Senegalese marabouts, as well as the ways in which they are performed, often through surrogate speech by a *géwël* or others who serve as intermediaries between speakers and their audiences. The texts thus constitute a dense field of cultural production that engages with the master discourses of Islam but which at the same time creates local meaning, much of which lies in the way in which the texts imbue a sense of authority for the marabout through their enactment of traditionalization, socialization of knowledge, and authorization.

Bibliography

Babou, Cheikh Anta. "Brotherhood Solidarity, Education and Migration: The Role of the Dahiras Among the Murid Muslim Community of New York." *African Affairs* 101 (2002): 151–70.

Bakhtin, Mikhail M. *The Dialogic Imagination.* Edited by Michael Holquist. Austin: University of Texas Press, 1981.

Barber, Karin. *The Anthropology of Texts, Persons and Publics: Oral and Written Culture in Africa and Beyond.* Cambridge: Cambridge University Press, 2007.

Bauman, Richard. *A World of Others' Words.* Malden, Mass.: Blackwell, 2004.

Buggenhagen, Beth Anne. "Beyond Brotherhood: Gender, Religious Authority, and the Global Circuits of Senegalese Muridiyya." In *New Perspectives on Islam in Senegal: Conversion, Migration, Wealth, Power and Femininity,* edited by Mamadou Diouf and Mara A. Leichtman, 189–210. New York: Palgrave, 2008.

Conrad, David C., and Barbara E. Frank, eds. *Status and Identity in West Africa: Nyamakalaw of Mande.* Bloomington: Indiana University Press, 1995.

Copans, Jean. *Les marabouts de l'arachide: La confrérie mouride et les paysans du Sénégal.* Paris: Le Sycomore, 1980.

Coulon, Christian. *Le marabout et le prince: Islam et pouvoir au Sénégal.* Paris: Pedone, 1981.

Cruise O'Brien, Donal B. *The Mourides of Senegal: The Political and Economic Organisation of an Islamic Brotherhood.* Oxford: Clarendon Press, 1971.

———. *Saints and Politicians: Essays in the Organisation of a Senegalese Peasant Society.* Cambridge: Cambridge University Press, 1975.

———. *Symbolic Confrontations: Muslims Imagining the State in Africa.* New York: Palgrave, 2003.

Dilley, Roy M. *Islamic and Caste Knowledge Practices Among Haalpulaar'en in Senegal.* Edinburgh: Edinburgh University Press, 2004.

Diop, Abdoulaye-Bara. *La société wolof, tradition et changement: Les systèmes d'inégalité et de domination.* Paris: Karthala, 1981.

Hale, Thomas A., and Paul Stoller. "Oral Art, Society, and Survival in the Sahel Zone." In *African Literature Studies: The Present State/l'état Present,* edited by Stephen Arnold, 163–69. Washington, D.C.: Three Continents Press, African Literature Association, and Institute for Research in Comparativc Literature, 1985.

Hoffman, Barbara G. *Griots at War: Conflict, Conciliation, and Caste in Mande.* Bloomington: Indiana University Press, 2000.

Irvine, Judith T. "Communication et société wolof à travers le temps et l'espace." In *Communication et société wolof: Héritage et création,* edited by Anna Diagne, Sascha Kesseler, and Christian Meyer. Paris: L'Harmattan, 2010.

———. "Shadow Conversations: The Indeterminacy of Participant Roles." In *Natural Histories of Discourse,* edited by Michael Silverstein and Greg Urban, 131–59. Chicago: University of Chicago Press, 1996.

Jansen, Jan. *The Griot's Craft.* Münster: Lit Verlag, 2000.

Janson, Marloes. *The Best Hand Is the Hand That Always Gives: Griottes and Their Profession in Eastern Gambia.* Leiden: CNWS Publications, 2002.

Mc Laughlin, Fiona. "'In the Name of God I Will Sing Again, Mawdo Malik the Good': Popular Music and the Senegalese Sufi *Tariqas.*" *Journal of Religion in Africa* 30, no. 2 (2000): 191–207.

———. "Islam and Popular Music in Senegal: The Emergence of a 'New Tradition.'" *Africa* 67, no. 4 (1997): 560–81.

Mc Laughlin, Fiona, and Leonardo A. Villalón. "Mettre en scène la légitimité: Un discours de feu Xalifa Abdoul Aziz Sy et de son *jottalikat.*" In *Communication et société Wolof: Héritage et création,* edited by Anna Diagne, Sascha Kesseler, and Christian Meyer, 303–27. Paris: L'Harmattan, 2010.

Panzacchi, Cornelia. The Livelihoods of Traditional Griots in Modern Senegal. *Africa* 64, no. 2 (1994): 190–210.

Robinson, David. *Paths of Accommodation: Muslim Societies and French Colonial Authorities in Senegal and Mauritania, 1880–1920.* Athens: Ohio University Press, 2000.

Tamari, Tal. *Les castes de l'Afrique occidentale: Artisans et musiciens endogames.* Nanterre: Société d'ethnologie, 1997.

Urban, Greg. "Entextualization, Replication, and Power." In *Natural histories of Discourse,* edited by Michael Silverstein and Greg Urban, 21–44. Chicago: University of Chicago Press, 1996.

Villalón, Leonardo A. "Generational Changes, Political Stagnation, and the Evolving Dynamics of Religion and Politics in Senegal." *Africa Today* 46, nos. 3–4 (1999): 129–47.

———. "Islamic Society and State Power in Senegal: Disciples and Citizens in Fatick." Cambridge: Cambridge University Press, 1995.

———. "Sufi Modernities in Contemporary Senegal: Religious Dynamics Between the Local and the Global." In *Sufism and the Modern in Islam,* edited by Martin van Bruinessen and Julia Day Howell, 172–91. London: I. B. Tauris, 2007.

———. "Sufi Rituals as Rallies: Religious Ceremonies in the Politics of Senegalese State-Society Relations." *Comparative Politics* 26 (1994): 414–37.

Wright, Bonnie L. "The Power of Articulation." In *Creativity of Power: Cosmology and Action in African Societies,* edited by W. Arens and I. Karp, 39–57. Washington, D.C.: Smithsonian Institution Press, 1989.

Yankah, Kwesi. *Speaking for the Chief: Okyeame and the Politics of Akan Royal Oratory.* Bloomington: Indiana University Press, 1995.

THE SUDANESE MAHDĪ'S ATTITUDES ON SLAVERY AND EMANCIPATION

Kim Searcy

ABSTRACT

The forces of the Sudanese Mahdī captured Khartoum in 1885 and brought an end to sixty-four years of Turco-Egyptian occupation of the Sudan. The Mahdī's revolt—from the perspective of many scholars of the period, such as P. M. Holt—was launched because of the Egyptian government's attempts to end slavery in the Sudan. This article analyzes the extant proclamations, sermons, and rulings of the Mahdī in order to identify his attitudes on slavery and emancipation. It argues that, contrary to what previous scholars have concluded, the Mahdī's revolt against the Turco-Egyptian forces was not motivated primarily by the suppression of the slave trade. Rather, the Mahdī responded to the occupation's imposition of poll taxes as a corrupted form of government divorced from the pure Islamic state he envisioned founding.

Introduction

The slave trade became a major commercial enterprise of the Sudanese economy in the nineteenth century. By 1877, this enterprise was the predominant occupation of the northern Sudanese. The Egyptian government's attempts to suppress this trade, from the late 1850s onwards, were largely unsuccessful. However, the abolition policies did affect many Sudanese and arguably laid the foundation for civil unrest and local revolts in the Sudan during the second half of the nineteenth century. For example,

Islamic Africa, VOL. 1, NO. 1, 2010. ISSN 2154-0993. www.islamicafricajournal.org

the suppression of the slave trade was a major factor in the revolts of 1878 that took place in Baḥr al-Ghazāl, Kordofan, and Dārfūr.[1] Abolition of the slave trade is also considered to be a major factor for the eruption of the most successful of these local revolts, the Mahdiyya.

This article argues that the writings of the leader of the Mahdiyya, Muḥammad Aḥmad al-Mahdī, reveal that his interest in slavery was peripheral in nature—contrary to what it was in the earlier revolts of 1878—and that his rebellion against the Egyptian government was solely motivated by religion. Muḥammad Aḥmad al-Mahdī, who henceforward will be referred to as the Mahdī, was neither an opponent nor a proponent of slavery; rather it was his sole desire to incorporate the institution of slavery within his vision of an Islamic theocracy. For instance, he simultaneously offered slaves "freedom in this world and paradise in the next" if they would fight under his standard, while he promised exemption to the slave traders if they would support his cause in its critical stages.[2]

The Mahdī was motivated to end what he viewed as the oppressive and corrupt Turco-Egyptian rule in the Sudan and to establish an Islamic state based upon the prophetic model. The foundation of the Mahdī's teachings focused on a return to the time of the nascent Islamic state in Medina in the seventh century. In addition, the Mahdī preached that he was going to "fill the earth with justice and piety just as it had been filled with tyranny and oppression." He also declared that those who offered their oath of allegiance to the Mahdiyya and pledged to support the war against the Egyptians would be included among the ranks of his followers. However, those who did not pledge their allegiance to the Mahdist cause would see that the Mahdī would wage war against them whether they were non-Muslim or Muslim.[3]

On one level, the Mahdī launched a revolt against the Turco-Egyptian occupiers because he wanted both to combat what he perceived as the irreligious practices of the occupiers and to revivify the religion of Islam in the Sudan, but on a more fundamental level he viewed the system of taxation imposed on the Sudanese by the Egyptian government as particularly

[1] Alice Moore-Harell, *Gordon and the Sudan: Prologue to the Mahdiyya, 1877–1880* (London: Frank Cass Publishers, 2001), 181.

[2] Na'um Shuqayr, *Ta'rīkh al Sūdān al-qadīm wa-l-ḥadīth wa-Jughrafiyatuhu,* ed. Muḥammad Abū Salīm (1967; repr., Beirut: Dār al Jīl, 1981), 315–20. Citations are to the 1967 edition.

[3] Ibid., 609.

oppressive and desired to put an end to this practice by defeating the occupiers militarily. Throughout the revolt, the Mahdī issued numerous proclamations and judgments on various subjects. The extant literature of this corpus has been edited and published in seven volumes by Muḥammad Ibrāhīm Abū Salīm under the title *Al-Āthār al kāmila li'l-Imām al-Mahdī* (The Complete Works of Imam al-Mahdī).[4] This article examines these sources in order to illuminate the Mahdī's attitudes on slavery, the slave trade, and emancipation.

In 1885, the Mahdiyya was successful in defeating the Turco-Egyptian forces that had occupied the Sudan since 1821. Muḥammad Aḥmad ibn 'Abd Allāh al-Mahdī claimed that he was al-Mahdī al-Muntaẓar, the "anticipated Deliverer." This appearance of the al-Mahdī al-Muntaẓar is one of the "signs of the hour" and is combined in Muslim eschatology with the second coming of Jesus.[5] Al-Mahdī al-Muntaẓar is a person who has a particular measure of divine guidance and is the repository of esoteric knowledge. It is his task, according to Muslim eschatological traditions, to "fill the earth with equity and justice, even as it has been filled with tyranny and oppression."[6] The Mahdī denounced the Turco-Egyptian government in the Sudan as being oppressive and religiously illegitimate and stated that God had designated him specifically to revitalize Islam in the Sudan and expel the Turco-Egyptian occupiers from the land.

In the leadership of the Mahdiyya his judgments and proclamations had the force of law. The Mahdī ignored all four "schools of law" (*madhāhib*). He claimed to base all of his rulings on the Qur'ān, Prophetic Sunna, and *ilhām* (inspiration). The Sunna as a source of law was more important than the Qur'ān because the Mahdī considered himself the successor to the Prophet Muḥammad. He claimed that he had the ability to communicate directly with the Prophet. Hence, *ilhām* ostensibly ranked higher than Hadith as a source of law for the Mahdī because it was impossible to doubt its authenticity as the Prophet himself was the transmitter. A transmitter of Hadith, on the contrary, can be declared untrustworthy. Thus, the Mahdī's

---

[4] Muḥammad Aḥmad al-Mahdī, *Al-Āthār al-kāmila li'l-imām al-Mahdī,* ed. Muḥammad Ibrāhīm Abū Salīm (Khartoum: Dār al-Wathā'iq, 1990), 5:417.

[5] Ahmad Ḥasan, trans., *Sunan Abū Dawūd* (Lahore: Sh. Muḥammad Ashrāf Publishers, 1984), 3:11190.

[6] Aharon Layish, "The Legal Methodology of the Mahdī in the Sudan, 1881–1885: Issues in Marriage and Divorce," *Sudanic Africa: A Journal of Historical Sources* 8 (1997): 37–66.

legal methodology permitted him to introduce innovations that were outside the purview of orthodox *sharī'a.*[7]

For instance, according to the *sharī'a,* slavery can only originate through captivity or birth. If a non-Muslim is not protected by a treaty and is captured by Muslims, then that individual can legally be enslaved. Furthermore, children born of two slaves, whether they are Muslim or not, assume the same servile status as their parents.[8] The Mahdī declared that the Turco-Egyptian occupiers of the Sudan were unbelievers and as such issued several rulings to his followers concerning how to dispose of Turco-Egyptian captives, whether to enslave them or to free them. These rulings occurred despite the fact that the majority of these captives were Muslims.

For example, during the early stages of the Mahdist revolt the Mahdī issued a proclamation stating that the Turco-Egyptians had rejected Islam and that if they did not surrender, their women and children were to be enslaved.

> When God's prophet, peace be upon him, appointed me as *al-mahdī,* He ordered me to wage jihād against the Turks. They are the worst people as far as unbelief and hypocrisy are concerned. They are intent upon extinguishing the light of God by insulting the *Sunnah* of the Prophet and weakening Islam. They have produced books, desiring with these books to extinguish the light of the Almighty. They call these books of law. They have placed you in shackles so that they can take your property, and wealth. In this they do not discriminate between the young or the old. So, do not abandon [the jihad] against them until they surrender their weapons, property and wealth to you. If they do this, do not enslave their women and children.[9]

This proclamation is an example of how the Mahdī used *ilhām* and *takfīr* (the charge of unbelief) to justify his war against his coreligionists. The prophet ordered him to wage war against the government because it had established policies that caused a great deal of suffering among the Sudanese. The Turco-Egyptians had established a new system of government

[7] Ibid.

[8] Joseph Schacht, *An Introduction to Islamic Law* (London: Oxford University Press, 1964), 127–28.

[9] Al-Mahdī, *Al-Āthār al-kāmila,* 5:417.

in the Sudan, one derived from the Ottoman administration. Their presence in the Sudan was purely exploitive in nature. They were colonizers who demanded obedience—the right to regulate affairs on every societal level—and claimed a right to extract a surplus for the Egyptian treasury.[10] The Mahdī in the above proclamation and in others of the same vein does not explicitly state how the Turco-Egyptian occupiers are damaging the religion. He merely hints that the reason for his denouncement of the administration is because the latter had appropriated the wealth and property of many of the Sudanese and introduced a new system of governance that had no relationship with Islam. The latter factor is what gave rise to the Mahdī's ire at the government. He maintained that the government was one steeped in unbelief and hypocrisy because the administrators, while claiming to be Muslims, were oppressing their fellow Muslims with their fiscal administrative polices. Throughout his proclamations, the Mahdī is adamant about declaring the Turco-Egyptians as infidels. Ostensibly, this is because he believed that those Muslims who oppressed their coreligionists were outside the purview of Islam.

Background to the Mahdīst Revolt

When the forces of the Mahdī defeated the Turco-Egyptian army at Khartoum on January 25, 1885, it signaled the end of a four-year revolt that brought to a close sixty years of Turco-Egyptian occupation of the Nilotic Sudan. Na'um Shuqayr, who worked for Turco-Egyptian intelligence during the Mahdist revolt, concluded that the Mahdiyya resulted from four causes: (1) the violence that accompanied the original Egyptian conquest of the Sudan in 1821, one that was still fresh in the memory of the people; (2) the partiality of the Turco-Egyptian occupying administration for certain tribes and Sufi orders; (3) the attempts of the government to suppress the slave trade; and (4) the levying of poll taxes on the populace.[11]

Peter M. Holt, who has written the most comprehensive history of the Mahdīst revolt to date, maintained that all the reasons provided by Shuqayr are valid, but not equally so. He maintained that the Egyptian government's attempts to end slavery created a sense of dissatisfaction that

---

[10] Anders Bjørkelo, *Prelude to the Mahdiyya: Peasants and Traders in the Shendi Region, 1821–1885* (Cambridge: Cambridge University Press, 1989), 34.

[11] Shuqayr, *Ta'rīkh al Sūdān*, 242.

transcended class and tribal affiliation in the Sudan and that ultimately led to the Mahdist revolt.[12]

There indeed was a general sense of dissatisfaction because of the manner in which Egypt attempted to suppress slavery. Egyptian-controlled regions in the Sudan expanded, with Egypt occupying and policing specific areas noted for their commerce in slaves. It is almost a certainty that many joined the Mahdist revolt because their livelihoods were threatened by the Egyptian policies to suppress the slave trade. For instance, ʻUthmān Diqna, an important commander in the Mahdist forces, was a well-established trader in slaves in the area of Suakin in the eastern Sudan before joining the Mahdist revolt. Furthermore, the Baqqāra Arabs in the area of Dārfūr in the west—some of the most notorious slave raiders in the Sudan—formed the military backbone of the Mahdīst forces. Hence, Holt's argument has merit.

However, the Mahdī's proclamations, *fatawā* (non-binding legal opinions), *khuṭab* (sermons), and *indharāt* (warnings) demonstrate that the issue of slavery was secondary to his plan to purify Islam in the Sudan. It was the levying of poll taxes that the Mahdī wrote most vehemently against in his proclamations. He contended that these taxes were *jizya* taxes, that is, taxes that Muslim governments required non-Muslim communities living within Muslim polities to pay. Hence, according to the Mahdī, these taxes were arbitrary and un-Islamic.

As stated above, the Mahdī called into question the religious legitimacy of the Turco-Egyptian regime. He maintained that, although they were operating under the guise of Islam, the occupiers were infidels because they were oppressing the Sudanese people by extracting surplus revenue for the government in the form of taxes.

> Verily, the Turks were imprisoning your men and placing them in chains. In addition, they were taking our women and children captive, and all of this was done for the sake of *jizya,* which was not sanctioned by the commands of God or His prophet. The Turks did not show any mercy to your children nor did they respect your elderly. How can you forget this? Has the zeal for God's religion not seized you?[13]

---

[12] P. M. Holt, *The Mahdist State in the Sudan: A Study of Its Origins, Development and Overthrow* (Oxford: Oxford University Press, 1958), 24.

[13] Al-Mahdī, *Al-Āthār al-kāmila,* 5:417.

The methods of taxation under the Turco-Egyptian administration became institutions that were feared by the populace. The collection of taxes was primarily a military operation. In addition, beatings and other forms of physical coercion were used on individuals who did not pay.[14]

Many Sudanese avoided paying the taxes by abandoning their homes and resettling in remoter regions where the authority of the government was weaker. The Mahdī thus viewed the imposition of the taxes on the Sudanese Muslim population as symbolic of the Turco-Egyptian regime's religious illegitimacy. The Mahdī regarded the policies of the Turco-Egyptian government as akin to unbelief and viewed the government and its administrators with the utmost disdain. Ostensibly, the imposition of these taxes from the Mahdī's perspective was an example of the introduction of imperial policies that underscored the oppressive and corrupt nature of the Turco-Egyptian government.

The designation "Turk" was applied by the Mahdī to those officials connected with the Turco-Egyptian regime regardless of ethnic origin. These officials were Egyptian, Armenian, or Circassian; one or two were Sudanese. The appellation "Turk" also suggested a lack of religious legitimacy because the "Turks" were considered non-Arab usurpers to the Caliphate. The Mahdī's legitimacy was based primarily on his claims of completely severing ties with the Turco-Egyptian government (known by the Sudanese as the Turkiyya) and the reestablishment of Islam in the Sudan based upon the prophetic model. Even captives of the Mahdī, such as Rudolf Slatin, were impressed with his ability to transform the religious practices of thc people:

> He (the Mahdī) preached renunciation; he had inveighed against earthly pleasures; he had broken down both social and official ranks; he had made rich and poor alike.[15]

The Mahdī claimed that his movement entailed a renewal and reinvigoration of the religion of Islam. This break with the past also entailed the abolition of all Sufi *ṭarīqa*s (orders) and all perceived religious innovations. The Turkiyya had favored certain Sufi orders and certain tribes,

---

[14] Bjørkelo, *Prelude to the Mahdiyya,* 89.

[15] Rudolf C. Slatin, *Fire and Sword in the Sudan* (1897; repr., London: Edward Arnold, 1905), 66. Citations are to the 1905 edition.

thus creating a social hierarchy that the Mahdī viewed as an un-Islamic innovation. From the Mahdī's perspective these innovations fostered by the Turkiyya resulted in a decline in the Sudanese people's devotion to Islam.

The Mahdī wrote a letter to a local religious leader, Sheikh 'Abd al-Fataḥ, in September 1880, expressing his concern about the condition of the religion at the time:

> It is well known that whosoever is for God and the establishment of His religion only finds ease in what is pleasing to God and will only live in a place where His religion is established. Innovation in the land has become widespread and the *'ulām'a* and the common people alike engage in it. . . . The only thing that remains of the Qur'ān is its form and the only thing that remains of Islam is its name.[16]

According to the Mahdī, the Qur'ān and Sunna should be the paradigm of behavior that every Muslim must follow. Everything else—such as the visitation of saints' tombs, excessive wailing at funerals, and Sufi orders—was considered by the Mahdī to be religious innovation. His writings are replete with references to his desire to purge Islam of the innovations that had entered the religion over time.

The Historical Context of Slavery in Egyptian-Sudanese Relations

The Mahdī considered the levying of poll taxes on the populace, as mentioned earlier, an innovation. These taxes were levied on the slave traders, their employees, and members of the population who had no connection to the slave trade but who lived in areas under Egyptian administrative domination. Shuqayr noted that the Sudanese people had no experience with the payment of regular taxes. In addition, he maintained that the taxes were not levied in an equitable manner; the poor had to pay more in taxes than their rich counterparts. The populace had to pay taxes on their houses, livestock, irrigated land, and agricultural products.[17] The tax burden was so great that by the mid-nineteenth century, many *jallāba* (itinerant traders)—most of whom were landless peasants—were forced into the slave trade.[18] Hence, slave trading in the mid-nineteenth century had become a

---

[16] Al-Mahdī, *Al-Āthār al-kāmila,* 2:51.

[17] Shuqayr, *Ta'rīkh al Sūdān,* 344.

[18] Moore-Harell, *Gordon and the Sudan,* 169.

very lucrative and widespread occupation for the northern Sudanese. The attempts of the Egyptian government to suppress the slave trade greatly impacted northern Sudan's economic lifeblood. Shuqayr noted that it was indeed the efforts to suppress the slave trade—rather than religious concerns—that propelled the Mahdī to raise the battle standard against the Turco-Egyptian regime.[19] Taj Hargey's thesis on the suppression of slavery in the Sudan echoes these sentiments: "The crippling tax demands gave rise to the Mahdist war cries of 'kill the Turks and cease to pay taxes,' and 'ten in one grave rather than a single dollar in taxes.'"[20] Al-Qaddāl adds that the tribes that were the most predominant in the Mahdīst revolt were those most affected economically by the Turkiyya's policies—the Baqqāra, Beja, Danāqla, and the Ja'liyīn.[21]

In August 1877, the Khedive Ismā'īl, who had succeeded to the vice-royalty of Egypt and its dependencies in 1863, concluded, with Great Britain, the Slave-Trade Convention. This agreement in theory ended the trade in Ethiopian and Sudanese slaves through Egyptian territory, and it also stipulated that private sale and purchase of slaves in the Sudan should end by 1889.

Despite ratifying the convention, the Khedive himself continued to use many slaves and eunuchs from the Sudan. He maintained close relations with powerful slave traders such as Abū Bakr, an Afar Somali, and with al-Zubayr Raḥma Mansūr, and the trade in slaves continued. As a consequence, the *jallāba* in both the Sudan and Egypt were reluctant to relinquish their hold on the trade that was providing them with their livelihood.

Furthermore, the provincial governors were reluctant to incur the ire of these merchants. As a consequence, these administrators merely read the proclamations condemning the slave trade but implemented no policy that would effectively put an end to it. The slave trade was an enterprise that no one in the Sudan or in Egypt had an interest in abolishing. Estimates place the number of slave traders in the Sudan in the 1860s and 1870s from 5,000 to 6,000 in the southern Sudan alone. The only measurable result the convention had on the slave trade was that it led to the increase in the price of slaves as part of the measures taken to suppress the trade. For example,

[19] Shuqayr, *Ta'rīkh al Sūdān,* 344.

[20] Taj Hargey, "The Suppression of Slavery in the Sudan, 1898–1939" (Ph.D. diss., Oxford University, 1982), 55.

[21] Muḥammad S. al-Qaddāl, *Al-Siyāsa al-iqtiṣādiyya fī-'l-Dawlat al-Mahdiyya* (Khartoum: Dār Jāmi'at al-Kharṭūm 1986), 50.

the price of a male slave in the 1820s had been around 10 Maria Theresa dollars; by 1879 it had increased to 30 of those dollars.[22]

The slave trade between Egypt and Sudan existed in antiquity and continued to thrive well into the Common Era. John S. Trimingham observed that the *baqṭ* agreement, a peace treaty between Arabian Muslims and Christian Nubians concluded in 656 CE, laid the foundation for trade between Nubia and Egypt, primarily in slaves.[23] The treaty lasted six hundred years, and for the most part the slaves came from the Upper Nile valley region.

The *jallāba,* on the eve of the Mahdiyya, were successful in capturing slaves because they possessed firearms that had been introduced to the country by Egypt. These slave traders, armed with rifles and pistols, enslaved blacks from the areas of the Upper Nile and Baḥr al-Ghazāl who were armed with the most rudimentary of weapons, spears, and swords. The largest provincial slave markets in proximity to where the actual raiding occurred were located in El-Obeid, Fashūda, and Qallābāt. The slave traders would purchase slaves from these regional markets and then sell them in the markets of Khartoum and Shendī, the two main northern markets. Most of these slaves were sent down the Nile to Egypt; others were ferried across the Red Sea to the Ḥijāz.[24]

It was not until the reign of the Khedive Ismā'īl that the Egyptian government began to implement policy that would end the slave trade. The Khedive appointed two British soldiers as governors of Equatoria to enforce the anti-slave-trade decrees. Samuel Baker served as governor from 1870 to 1873, and Charles Gordon from 1874 to 1879. These men managed to curtail the slave trade to a certain degree, but since it was so entrenched in the Sudan at the time, it was difficult for it to be completely eliminated. In addition, the Egyptian government, even though enacting policy to abolish the slave trade, continued to obtain its soldiers from this commerce. Slaves apprehended by the Egyptian forces were forced into military service.[25] The majority of these slaves came from the Nūba Mountains and was known as the *jihādiyya.* The slave trade, despite the pressure the British government placed upon the Egyptian rulers to abolish it, never completely ended.

---

[22] Moore-Harrell, *Gordon and the Sūdan,* 129.

[23] J. S. Trimingham, *Islam in the Sūdan* (London: Frank Cass and Co., 1949), 62.

[24] Shuqayr, *Ta'rīkh al-Sūdān,* 250.

[25] Ibid.

The Mahdī's Rulings on Slaves and Slavery

The Mahdī's proclamations are replete with the theme that the Turco-Egyptian regime was steeped in unbelief because of its imposition of taxes on, and oppression of, the Muslim Sudanese. Thus as far as the Mahdī was concerned, it became incumbent upon the Sudanese Muslims to take up arms against the oppressors and dispose of the spoils of war in a religiously sanctioned manner. The Mahdī wrote a letter in November 1883 to 'Ata al-Manan, informing the latter of how the spoils of war should be divided.

> The booty must be divided into fifths. A fifth is to be deposited into the Public Treasury (Bayt al-Māl) and the remainder is to be divided amongst the army. . . . Free people should not be enslaved, with the exception of the Turks. Their men and women are booty of war.[26]

The Mahdī instituted several economic reforms during the revolt, one of which was the establishment of the Bayt al Māl. Despite its English translation, the Bayt al Māl was not merely a treasury. All weapons, gold, horses, prisoners of war, silver, and slaves were to be handed over to the public treasury. One-fifth was given to the Mahdī, and the remainder was distributed amongst the Mahdist forces.[27] All war booty, confiscated property, and fines for theft and drinking were collected in the public treasury. In addition to the repository of war booty and collected taxes, the public treasury also served as a public slave auction house.

Slaves were sold in the treasury, and a written certificate was given to the purchaser stating in detail the description of the slave. Thus it becomes evident from the existence of this public treasury that the Mahdī had no qualms with slavery and the commerce in slaves as long as it was carried out in what he claimed to be an Islamically sanctioned manner.

Islam does not prohibit slavery—thus, the Mahdī could have argued successfully that the Khedive's attempts to end the slave trade and slavery were an un-Islamic innovation because God and His Prophet permitted the practice. However, it seems that the Mahdī viewed all of the Turkiyya's

---

[26] Al-Mahdī, *Al-Āthār al-kāmila,* 3:439.

[27] Anders Bjørkelo and Ahmad Ibrahīm Abū Shouk, eds., *The Public Treasury of the Muslims: Monthly Budgets of the Mahdist State in the Sudan, 1897* (Leiden, E. J. Brill, 1996), xxvii.

policies as innovations, slavery and the slave trade included. As a consequence, he ostensibly strived to refashion the institution based upon the *sharīʿa.*

The Mahdī wrote to Asākir Abū Kalām, the chief of the Jimiʿ people, in June 1882, informing him of a man from the Dār Ḥamid tribe whom the Mahdī declared had died in a state of unbelief. The Mahdī ruled that since this man was an unbeliever, "his property, children and women were to be handed over to the Public Treasury of the Muslims."[28] According to the *sharīʿa,* a non-Muslim who is not protected by a treaty is in a state of war, and his life and property are unprotected. Hence, by declaring the man an unbeliever, the Mahdī made it permissible for the dead man's children and wives to be legally enslaved. It is not clear what sort of occurrence occasioned the Mahdī's pronouncement of unbelief on the man. However, as noted earlier, the Mahdī had announced on several occasions that the Turks had rejected Islam. Ostensibly the dead man, although not a Turk, may have been conniving with them in some manner. Thus, those individuals or groups who opposed the Mahdī were subject to being declared as unbelievers. Conversely, individuals or groups who were followers of the Mahdī were afforded the highest degree of legal rights.

Prior to the Mahdiyya it was commonplace for the Baqqāra tribes in the area of Kordofan and Dārfūr to engage in raids against one another and to enslave the women and children captured, despite the fact that they were Muslims. In December 1882, the Mahdī commanded the tribe of the Banū Ḥussayn and the followers of ʿAṭa al-Manan to end their hostilities against each other and to end the enslavement of the women taken in these raids.[29] In addition, the Mahdī ordered his followers among the nomadic Baqqāra tribes to desist in raids in the regions inhabited by the Shilluk in the area of southern Kordofan. As noted earlier, these regions had been one of the chief sources for slaves during the Turkiyya. The Mahdī ordered that these practices end because they threatened the unity of the Mahdiyya. Moreover, he had forged alliances with non-Muslim groups to advance his movement. The Mahdī concluded a treaty with a chief of the Shilluk whereby the chief and his followers became participants in the Mahdiyya, thus ending slave raiding in that particular region. The Mahdī wrote the following proclamation to his followers in December 1883:

---

[28] Al-Mahdī, *Al-Āthār al-kāmila,* 1:133.

[29] Ibid., 2:261.

> Indeed the Shilluk have chosen to join you and become united with you. . . . A group of men among them are coming to us for the sake of taking the oath of allegiance (*Bay'a*) and negotiation. After this is concluded, it is necessary for us to construct a mosque for them so that they can pray and teach them how to make ablutions, and teach [the women] to dress Islamically. In addition we will teach them the Mahdī's prayer book (*al-Rātib*) and how to recite the first chapter of the Qur'ān (Al-Fātiḥa) if possible. We will encourage them to always remember God. Also we will designate a holy man from among us to serve as their Imam.[30]

Apparently, after this proclamation was issued, raiding continued in the Shilluk region, because the Mahdī issued another proclamation in February 1884, to the Baqqāra living in the region. The Mahdī ordered the nomads to end all hostilities against the Shilluk and to treat them in a harmonious manner.[31]

The acceptance of the Shilluk as allies in the Mahdiyya underscores the utter contempt the Mahdī had for the Turks as Muslims. He was willing to accept non-Muslims as compatriots provided they offered their oath of allegiance to the Mahdiyya while continuing to excoriate the Turks.

In the same month and year he issued the ruling on the dead man of the Dār Ḥamid, the Mahdī issued another ruling concerning a boy who had been captured by some marauding Bedouins in the territory of the Jimi' people on the White Nile, northeast of the Nūba Mountains. The Bedouins had handed over the boy to the Jimi' chief Asākir Abū Kalām, whom the Mahdī wrote demanding the boy's release.

> Praise be to God and pray for our prophet Muḥammad and his family. From the servant of his lord, Muhḥammad al-Mahdī ibn Sayyid 'Abd Allāh to our beloved in God Shaykh Asākir Abū Kalām: Al-Bashīr walad Daw al-Bayt came to us and informed us that his son had been stolen by some Bedouins and handed over to you. The boy is now [in your territory]. O my beloved, verily the boy is free . . . and indeed whosoever possesses a free person [as a slave], God will fight him on the last day. You have signed a treaty with us and you are a follower of the Qur'ān and *Sunnah,* thus release the aforementioned son of al-Bashīr without delay or hindrance. Indeed, the boy is one of our followers and a disciple. He

[30] Ibid., 2:262.

[31] Ibid., 2:278.

> emigrated with us, thus his hardship is our hardship and his contentment is our contentment. Peace.[32]

These rulings illustrate the manner in which Mahdī dealt with the issue of slavery in regards to the position of non-Muslims vis-à-vis Muslims. The basis of the Islamic attitude towards unbelievers is that they must be either converted, subjugated, or killed with the exception of women, children, and slaves. War captives are either enslaved or left alive as free *dhimmī*s.[33] Those non-Muslims—such as the Shilluk, who concluded a treaty with the Mahdī—were free of the above conditions provided they remained steadfast in their support of the Mahdiyya.

The Mahdī's proclamations, however, are muted on the subject of the Turco-Egyptian government's policies concerning the suppression of the slave trade. His rulings primarily address the condition of slaves and the proper way to buy and sell them. For example, in a letter penned on January 11, 1883, the Mahdī ordered his uncle, Maḥmūd 'Abd al-Qādir, to sell a slave and establish the price of the slave in a religiously sanctioned manner.[34]

In May of the same year, the Mahdī, responding to the news that several children of his followers had been kidnapped and subsequently enslaved by nomads, wrote a proclamation condemning this action and requested that the perpetrators be apprehended.[35]

In the summer of 1883, the Mahdī issued a proclamation requiring his followers to engage in trade in the manner sanctioned by the Qur'ān and Sunna. He made explicit his desire for the implementation of the *sharī'a*-sanctioned manner of carrying out commerce with the following proclamation:

> God the most high has made it clear for you that you must be honest in buying and selling in all of your dealings. . . . Do not deceive and do not lie. Whosoever does so is not one of us.[36]

---

[32] Al-Mahdī, *Al-Āthār al-kāmila,* 1:134. This emigration the Mahdī is referring to is the departure of the Mahdist forces from Abā Island to the Nūba Mountains in the autumn of 1881.

[33] Schacht, *Introduction to Islamic Law,* 127.

[34] Al-Mahdī, *Al-Āthār al-kāmila,* 1:235.

[35] Ibid., 1:294.

[36] Joseph Ohrwalder, *Ten Years Captivity in the Mahdī's Camp, 1883–1892* (London: William Clowes and Sons, 1892), 208.

Implicit in this proclamation is a directive on the Islamic ally-based manner to buy and sell slaves as well. Consequently, the Mahdī was calling for consistency in regards to the issue of the proper disposal of slaves. This call for consistency is further emphasized in regard to the question of what should become of Muslim captives. It was noted above that the Mahdī ordered that if the Turks did not surrender, then their women and children should be enslaved. Some of the Mahdī's warriors had enslaved Turkish women captured in battle. After their capture these women, most of whom were Muslims, were used as concubines and on rare occurrences domestic servants. This prompted the Mahdī to issue a *fatwā* on November 1882, exhorting his followers to abandon this practice.

> We have informed all of the brothers against greed for booty. . . . Everything you find must be collected save weapons and sent to me. The Muslim women included. If they are captured do not sell them into slavery. For whoever does this is not one of us.[37]

According to, Shuqayr, the women were distributed amongst the Mahdī and his commanders.[38] Thus, it seems that the warriors were enslaving these women and utilizing them for their own interests instead of handing them over to the public treasury.

The Mahdī's revolt eliminated the influence of many of the large slave-trading companies in the Sudan. Furthermore, the Mahdists took relatively few slaves in comparison to the raids that were carried out during the Turkiyya.[39] But this does not suggest that the Mahdī was adverse to slavery or the slave trade. On the contrary, in a general proclamation written in the winter of 1883, the Mahdī issued an order to his followers that they not neglect mundane matters such as recapturing runaway slaves and stray animals.[40] He also wrote around the same time to the sheikh of the Kabābīsh, Ṣāliḥ wad Faḍlallāh, to his brother al-Ṭūm, and to Alī wad Quraysh, ordering that they return the slaves and other properties they had

---

[37] Al-Mahdī, *Al-Āthār al-kāmila,* 1:197.

[38] Shuqayr, *Ta'rīkh al Sūdān,* 537.

[39] Robert O. Collins, "The Nilotic Sudan," in *The Human Commodity: Perspectives on the Trans-Saharan Slave Trade,* ed. Elizabeth Savage, 150 (London: Frank Cass and Co., 1992).

[40] Al-Mahdī, *Al-Āthār al-kāmila,* 1:281.

taken in a raid from Dafa'a Allāh wad Muḥammad al-Juhaynī in the western Sudan.[41]

After the fall of Khartoum in January 1885, the number of slaves found in the city had increased dramatically. The director (*amīn*) of the Bayt al-Māl at the time, Aḥmad Sulaymān, wrote a letter to the Mahdī in February 1885, complaining that the expenditure of funds from the treasury for the maintenance of these slaves had become exorbitant. As a consequence, he wanted to know what should be done with the slaves. Should they be sold or distributed among the army? In response, the Mahdī wrote a letter to the Khalīfa 'Abdallāhī, the second-in-command of the Mahdist forces, informing the latter that the slaves should be distributed among the army.[42]

A proportion of the Mahdist forces comprised slave soldiers, the *jihādiyya,* who were captured in the Mahdiyya's battles with the Turks. A month after the fall of Khartoum the Mahdī ordered that the *jihādiyya* in Khartoum should be divided and that each Mahdist commander should receive twenty members of this force.[43] The *jihādiyya* played a major role in the Mahdiyya's military successes because they were highly trained soldiers skilled in the use of firearms.

According to Holt, however, the Mahdiyya's success can primarily be attributed to an alliance of three elements all of which were opposed to the Turkiyya. The Mahdī and his original disciples were the core group. This group was noted for its piety. The second group comprised the *jallāba,* who were discontent due to the suppression of the slave trade. Members of the Mahdī's family, the Ashrāf, were part of this group. The third group was the Baqqāra nomads of the west who desired an end to taxation and the acquisition of booty.[44] Holt added that the Mahdī's proclamations against concealing booty and the measures taken to enforce the payment of *zakāh* (alms tax) illustrated the laxity with which the Baqqāra viewed their duties as members of the Mahdiyya.[45] This laxity also extended to the Mahdī's relatives. For instance, the Mahdī wrote a letter to his cousin al-Muqaddam Muḥammad on June 7, 1885, declaring that some of the Ashrāf had taken into their possession slaves not owned by

---

[41] Ibid.

[42] Al-Mahdī, *Al-Āthār al-kāmila,* 4:305.

[43] Ibid., 4:284

[44] Holt, *Mahdīst State in the Sudan,* 118.

[45] Ibid.

them. The Mahdī ordered that the slaves be returned to their original owners.[46]

The Mahdī died unexpectedly two weeks after issuing this proclamation, and it is evident that in this proclamation and the others treating the issue of slaves and slavery, the Mahdī did not abolish any of the immutable laws; rather, he added several precepts that lent a decidedly Mahdīst hue to the *sharī'a.* He maintained the parameters of Islamic law while legislating laws to fit his own vision of an Islamic state; thus, his proclamations on slavery must be interpreted in this context.

The Mahdī maintained that the Turks' presence had caused the deterioration of religion in the Sudan and that he alone had a divine mandate to rule and legislate laws.

The Mahdī claimed that the Prophet appeared to him in visions, exhorting all to recognize his authority: "Whosoever does not believe in the Mahdī is an infidel in the eyes of God and His prophet."[47] These visions of the Prophet, in addition to the Qur'ān and Sunna, formed the basis of the Mahdī's proclamations, and as such they had the force of law behind them. In Islamic law, legal concepts are fused with religious meaning. The Qur'ānic precepts and Sunna are immutable standards. Traditional *sharī'a* is a kind of divine civil law; however, the Mahdī employed the law to emphasize the legitimacy of the Mahdiyya and continuously call into question the religious legitimacy of the Turco-Egyptian government. Hence, in relationship to slavery, the Mahdī was implying that the Turkiyya's approach to the institution was not in accordance with Islamic law. As noted above, wanton kidnapping and enslavement of Muslims by fellow Muslims during the Turkiyya were what the Mahdī was forced to address in his proclamations. The Mahdī desired to end practices such as these in order to attain his goal of establishing an Islamic theocracy based upon the nascent Muslim state in Medina.

The Mahdī's Rulings on Manumission

The manumission of slaves is recommended in Islam. In certain instances it is prescribed as a religious expiation. For example, in July 1884, the

[46] Al-Mahdī, *Al-Āthār al-kāmila,* 5:167.

[47] Muḥammad Aḥmad al-Mahdī, *Manshūrāt al-Mahdiyyah,* ed. Muḥammad Ibrahīm Abū Salīm (Khartoum: Dār al-Wathā'iq, 1969), 14.

Mahdī issued a proclamation prohibiting the physical greeting between men and women. Anyone breaking this law could be punished by receiving fifty lashes from a whip or forced to fast two consecutive months, or in lieu of this, emancipate a slave.[48]

The Mahdī issued several rulings concerning manumission. For instance, in May 1884, the Mahdī issued a *fatwā* concerning a concubine who had given birth to a child of her master. The child subsequently died, and the master separated from the concubine. The concubine continued to serve as a servant to her master but gave birth to a child with another slave. The Mahdī ruled that the concubine and her child should be freed.[49] This ruling seems to be an innovation of the *sharī'a* stipulation concerning a category of concubine known as *umm walad.* The *umm walad* is a female slave who has given birth to a child of her owner which he has recognized.

The issue of emancipation was raised again in April of the following year. Al-Ṭayyib al-Bannānī, a Moroccan from Fez who was traveling in Berber in the northern Sudan, had his property taken as booty by the Mahdī's followers in the region. The Moroccan's property included emancipated slaves, one of which was the maternal uncle of his children. Al-Bananī wrote to the Mahdī, having the latter issue a ruling to get his slaves returned to him. On May 6, the Mahdī commanded that the emancipated slaves should be returned to the Moroccan.[50]

After the capture of Khartoum, the Mahdiyya began to undergo a transformation from a revolutionary movement to that of an established state. Thus, the Mahdī's role as legislator and interpreter of the *sharī'a* became even more pronounced. In May 1885, Muḥammad Sulaymān, the commander of the Dārfūrian *jihādiyya,* wrote to the Mahdī asking his advice concerning whether it was permissible to emancipate a concubine who had been a slave of the Turks for eight years. The concubine's brother brought her from the region of Dār Fūr where she was enslaved. The brother was able to locate his sister, and he wanted the condition of servitude to be lifted from her. Muḥammad Sulaymān wrote that he did not believe the concubine should be emancipated because "if we open this door, [concerning the frequent request of freeing slaves] we will never be able to close it again.[51] The Mahdī responded in the following manner:

[48] Al-Mahdī, *Al-Āthār al-kāmila,* 3:109.

[49] Ibid., 3:70.

[50] Ibid., 4:476.

[51] Ibid., 4:381.

I addressed this issue when we were in El-Obeid. The door is closed [on the issue]. If she was enslaved during the Mahdiyya, then she is free. Peace.[52]

During this period, the Mahdī had to issue several proclamations concerning the status of property during the conquest of Khartoum. Apparently, a great deal of looting had occasioned the conquest, and slaves were included in the property that was taken. According to Rudolf Slatin, slaves frequently ran away from their masters and were recaptured and sold by others as their own property. Thus, the theft of slaves was a common practice after the fall of Khartoum. "They were frequently enticed into other people's houses, or secretly induced to leave the fields, then thrown into chains and carried off."[53] It was due to this theft of slaves that the Mahdī, shortly after the conquest of Khartoum, issued a proclamation commanding his followers to return all slaves that had been taken unlawfully, that is, slaves who were not captured in battle.[54]

The slaves who were captured lawfully and auctioned for sale in the nascent Mahdist state were in great demand. Slatin notes that there was an almost daily sale in slaves.[55] The people of Berber and the Ja'liyīn, a riverine people, complained that they wished to purchase slaves, but the price was too dear. As a consequence, the Mahdī ruled that the price should be lowered on the slaves to allow these people the opportunity to purchase them.[56]

During the Mahdī's short rule as leader of the Mahdist state (he died six months after the conquest of Khartoum), his proclamations and *fatāwā* are relatively silent concerning the emancipation of slaves. While Islam retains the institution of slavery under certain conditions, some Muslim scholars claim that Islam encourages the liberation of slaves. Despite this claim, the liberation of slaves in all Muslim polities throughout the ages was a rare occurrence. The Mahdiyya was no exception to this rule. For instance, the Mahdī decreed that the emancipation of a slave could be used as a form of punishment for a slave master's contravention of a rule of law of the Mahdīst state.[57]

---

52 Ibid. The city of El-Obeid fell to the Mahdist forces in January 1883.

53 Slatin, *Fire and Sword,* 536.

54 Al-Mahdī, *Al-Āthār al-kāmila,* 5:167.

55 Slatin, *Fire and Sword,* 536.

56 Ibid.

57 Al-Mahdī, *Al-Āthār al-kāmila,* 4:190.

Conclusion

From these his writings, it seems clear that the Mahdī did not wish the commerce in slaves or slavery to end. Rather, he advocated a restructuring of the institution under the auspices of the Mahdiyya. These proclamations and *fatwā* of the Mahdī indicate that he was neither an opponent of slavery and the slave trade nor an advocate of emancipation.

The Mahdī's writings do not reveal that it was the Turkiyya's attempts to end slavery in the Sudan that propelled him to engage in a revolt against the regime. The Mahdī's attitudes concerning slavery indicate that he desired to restructure it in a manner suited to his visions of an Islamic state. The Mahdiyya was a revolt against Turco-Egyptian rule in the Sudan. The Mahdī denounced the government as tyrannical, oppressive, and un-Islamic because it had introduced policies that resulted in privations for many of the northern Sudanese. Additionally, the Mahdī maintained that he was sent to end the injustice and oppression that the Sudanese had been experiencing at the hands of the occupying Turco-Egyptian regime.

This is the reason why, throughout his proclamations, the Mahdī mentions the levying of taxes on the populace. The Mahdī viewed the levying of taxes as an un-Islamic innovation of the Turco-Egyptian government. Furthermore, this policy of the Turkiyya, although cutting across all class and tribal divisions in the northern Sudan, primarily affected the largest segment of Sudanese society, the peasants, who ultimately were responsible for providing the greatest support to the Mahdiyya.

Bibliography

Bjørkelo, Anders. *Prelude to the Mahdiyya: Peasants and Traders in the Shendi Region, 1821–1885.* Cambridge: Cambridge University Press, 1989.

Bjørkelo, Anders, and Aḥmad Ibrāhīm Abū Shouk, eds. *The Public Treasury of the Muslims: Monthly Budgets of the Mahdist State in the Sudan, 1897.* Leiden, E. J. Brill, 1996.

Collins, Robert O. "The Nilotic Sudan." In *The Human Commodity: Perspectives on the Trans-Saharan Slave Trade,* edited by Elizabeth Savage, 140–61. London, England: Frank Cass and Co., 1992.

Hargey, Taj. "The Suppression of Slavery in the Sudan, 1898–1939." Ph.D. diss., Oxford University, 1982.

Ḥasan, Aḥmad, trans. *Sunan Abū Dawūd.* 3 vols. Lahore: Sh. Muḥammad Ashrāf Publishers, 1984.

Holt, P. M. *Mahdīst State in the Sudan: A Study of its Origins, Development and Overthrow.* Oxford: Oxford University Press, 1958.

Layish, Aharon. "The Legal Methodology of the Mahdī in the Sudan, 1881–1885: Issues in Marriage and Divorce." *Sudanic Africa: A Journal of Historical Sources* 8 (1997): 37–66.

al-Mahdī, Muḥammad Aḥmad. *Al-Āthār al-kāmila li'l-imām al-Mahdī.* Edited by Muḥammad Ibrahīm Abū Salīm. 7 vols. Khartoum: Dār al-Wathā'iq, 1990.

al-Mahdī, Muḥammad Aḥmad. *Manshūrāt al-Mahdiyyah.* Edited by Muḥammad Abū Salīm. Khartoum: Dār al-Wathā'iq, 1969.

Moore-Harell, Alice. *Gordon and the Sudan: Prologue to the Mahdiyya, 1877–1880.* London: Frank Cass Publishers, 2001.

al-Qaddāl, Muḥammad S. *Al-Siyāsa al-iqtisādiyya fī- 'l-Dawlat al-Mahdiyya.* Khartoum: Dār Jāmi'at al-Kharṭūm, 1986.

Schacht, Joseph. *Introduction to Islamic Law.* Oxford: Oxford University Press, 1964.

Shuqayr, Na'um. *Ta'rīkh al Sūdān al-qadīm wa-l-ḥadīth wa-Jughrafiyatuhu.* Edited by Muḥammad Abū Salīm. Beirut: Dar al-Thaqāfa, 1967. Reprint, Beirut: Dār al Jīl, 1981. Page references are to the 1967 edition.

Slatin, Rudolf C. *Fire and Sword in the Sudan.* 1897. Reprint, London: Edward Arnold, 1897. Page references are to the 1905 edition.

Trimingham, J. S. *Islam in the Sudan.* London: Frank Cass and Co., 1949.

LIBYA, THE TRANS-SAHARAN TRADE OF EGYPT, AND 'ABDALLAH AL-KAHHAL, 1880–1914

Terence Walz

Egypt's trans-Saharan trade along its western frontier with Libya underwent perceptible changes in the course of the nineteenth century. The development of strong commercial ties with the kingdom of Darfur during the previous century and the implantation of an imperial regime in the eastern Sudan, beginning in 1820, dramatically changed the direction of trade with Black Africa, away from the western Sudan toward the east. During most of the nineteenth century, Egypt drew heavily on the resources of what is now present-day Sudan for supplies of slaves, ivory, feathers, gum, and other products of the trans-Saharan African export market.[1]

The "western route," originating in such entrepôts as Katsina, Kano, and Kukuwa, and in new markets in Abeche and Wara, traversed the deserts of Libya via the oasis towns of Murzuq, Awjila and Jalu, passing eastward through the Egyptian oasis of Siwa before halting at various small villages outside Cairo in the vicinity of the Pyramids. Trade along this route, dormant in the early part of the nineteenth century, revived in spasms, apparently as a result of periodic efforts by sultans of Wadai to open up commerce with the north. It fell under the control of the Majabra,

[1] This article was originally presented as "Libya, the Transsaharan Trade of Egypt, and 'Abd Allah al-Kahhal, 1880–1914," at the First International Conference on Trans-Saharan Trade, Libyan Studies Center, Tripoli, Libya, in September 1979. It was originally published in Arabic as Terence Walz, "Tijarat al-qawafil bayn Libya wa Misr," in *Majallat al-buhuth al-Tarikhiyya* (Tripoli, Libya) 1 (1981): 89–113.

Islamic Africa, VOL. 1, NO. 1, 2010. ISSN 2154-0993. www.islamicafricajournal.org

intrepid merchants of Jalu oasis, who established trading communities in Egypt and Benghazi as well as in Murzuq and Abeche. The Egyptian end of the route became more active sometime during the 1860s, for already by 1871 European observers in Cairo were noting the existence of a "new" depot for African goods at Kirdasa, a village on the western edge of the Delta, some eight kilometers from Cairo.[2]

In comparison with the volume of trade passing through southern Egypt from the Sudan, both from Khartoum and from the independent kingdom of Darfur, the volume of the western trade was insignificant. However, two important political events changed this situation. The long-projected Egyptian conquest of Darfur, carried out in 1874, effectively killed the trade along the Darb al-Arba'in, a route connecting that kingdom with Asyût, the capital of Upper Egypt. The organization of large caravans had been a state function, and with the removal of the Fur sultan and royal patronage, supplies of ivory, gum, feathers, and tamarind—as well as slaves, whose import was by then illegal—dried up. The new Egyptian administration proved incapable of reconstituting the trade, and certainly by the 1890s, the once-busy markets of African goods in Asyût had fallen silent.

On the other hand, the decade of the 1870s saw steady, even spectacular, increases in exports from the Egyptian Sudan. This is borne out in the records of British customhouses, particularly in the records of gum imports that showed a jump from 44,609 cwt. in 1874 to 76,702 cwt. in 1882. The export from Egypt of ivory, which went almost entirely to Britain, and of feathers, of which only a percentage went to Britain (the largest share being absorbed by France), presents problems for analysis, and it is possible that the loss of the Darfur contributed to the unsteadiness of their supply since ivory and feathers were major Darfur exports before the Egyptian conquest.

The impact of the triumph of Mahdism in the Sudan can be seen in British customs records. A bumper ivory export figure of 2,835 cwt. in 1883 is followed by a paltry 404 cwt. the following year—this being the year that the Mahdi encircled Khartoum. Feather exports in 1883 amounted to

[2] Background may be found in Terence Walz, *Trade between Egypt and Bilad as-Sudan, 1700–1820* (Cairo: Institut français d'archéologie orientale du Caire, 1978); "Notes on the Organization of the African Trade in Cairo, 1800–1850," *Annales islamologiques* 9 (1972): 263–86; "Asyut in the1260s A.H. (1944–53)," *Journal of the American Research Center in Egypt* 15 (1978): 113–26; Dennis Cordell, "Eastern Libya, Wadai and the Sanusiya: A Tariqa and a Trade Route," *Journal of African History* 18, no. 1 (1977): 1. He dates the increase to the 1860s.

13,349 lb., while in 1884 they declined to 4,396 lb., and in 1885 to 383 lb. Gum exports fell from 76,702 cwt. in 1882 to 40,692 cwt. in the following year and to 17,676 cwt. in 1884. The liberation of the Sudan from foreign control also isolated it from foreign markets, and throughout the duration of the Mahdiyya, trade with Egypt was either officially prohibited or drastically reduced. The Mahdiyya ended in 1898 when the Anglo-Egyptian rule was militarily imposed.

Both official Egyptian and British records show that while greatly diminished, Sudan goods were not altogether eliminated. This may be seen in Table 1, which has been compiled on the basis of the more complete

TABLE 1
British Imports from Egypt, 1880–1899

Year	Ivory Cwts	Value	Feathers lbs	Value	Gum cwt	Value	Total Value
1880	2,003	74,850	22,990	26,770	51,543	149,021	250,641
1881	1,243	46,640	3,803	5,789	72,403	182,084	234,504
1882	92	4,166	8,748	11,331	76,702	168,646	184,143
1883	2,835	114,519	13,349	10,825	40,692	92,028	217,372
1884	404	16,500	4,396	4,700	18,676	68,002	89,202
1885	13	680	383	2,450	14,967	75,335	78,465
1886	482	18,192	595	1,003	7,131	38,858	58,053
1887	100	4,927	2,402	2,651	6,548	32,812	40,390
1888	309	13,450	590	495	2,247	11,506	25,451
1889	2	50	636	820	2,359	12,455	13,325
1890	537	23,360	784	500	1,424	8,402	32,232
1891	15	600	2,392	2,310	1,824	9,547	12,457
1892	47	1,855	392	230	6,458	25,370	27,455
1893	58	1,870	855	810	7,225	25,191	27,871
1894	328	9,615	1,581	1,212	4,817	20,345	31,172
1895	80	3,430	5,243	4,959	11,095	36,105	44.494
1896	81	2,768	4,184	3,560	10,252	33,846	40,174
1897	18	700	4,922	3,750	2,212	7,397	11,847
1898	51	1,560	7,153	6,755	3,705	12,693	21,008
1899	151	5,780	9,360	7,175	8,184	27,613	40,568

Source: Public Records Office, London, CUST 5/123-161, 1880–1899

I am grateful to Christopher Steed, School of Oriental and African Studies, London, for his assistance in obtaining this information.

records of British customhouses. Our knowledge of the sources for Sudan goods during the period 1885–99 remains inexact, but these sources are nonetheless interesting because they provide evidence of trade during a period of great political disturbance. Supplies may have seeped in through the embargoed Mahdist Sudan or may have originated in Sawakin, which the Egyptians retained; the greater probability is that they were brought from the western Sudan and entered Egypt via Libya and the Egyptian western frontier.

This article focuses on that western portion of Egypt's trade with Sudanic Africa during the last decade of the nineteenth century and early years of the twentieth. In order to dramatize the trade and how it functioned, the paper has been cast in terms of a biographical portrait of ʻAbdallah al-Kahhal (ca. 1840–1921), who personified Egypt's intra-African connections. His role as a merchant, agent, and government confidant reveals in unusual ways the nature of the trade and its interests and quirks. ʻAbdallah al-Kahhal's career spans foreign occupation, religious and nationalist revival, and empire building. He was connected, in one degree or another, with the Mahdists, the Sanusiyya, Rabih ibn Fadlallah, the sultans of Wadai, and British officialdom in Cairo. His life exemplifies the meshing of politics and commerce and the dynamic role Egypt plays with its African neighbors.

ʻAbdallah al-Kahhal: Beginnings

ʻAbdallah al-Kahhal was born in Damascus around 1840, the son of Muhi al-Din al-Kahhal. He went to the Sudan in his early thirties, settling in Khartoum that was then enjoying a boom time. Sudan's export trade was largely in the hands of a select number of Egyptians and Syrians who had the confidence of the government and who operated, in some cases, with the aid of European capital.[3] Chief among the Egyptian merchants were the al-ʻAqqad and al-Siyufi families, with headquarters in Cairo and close links with the khedivial establishment. The Coptic merchant Shanuda was also important. Among the Syrian houses were the Luftallah,

[3] Partnership between Cassavetes and Company, Maximos Sakkakini, Keriaku Christodolo and Company, Andrea Debono, Ahmad Rafa'i al-ʻAqqad, and Musa Hasan al-ʻAqqad, dated 26 Dhu'l-Hijja 1278/24 June 1862, Public Record Office (PRO), Foreign Office 841/29, file 1, letter no. 9. The capital amounted to 2,800,000 piastres, which was placed in the hands of the al-ʻAqqads.

Farajallah, Rizqallah al-Jadd, Na'um Sukar, Jirjis al-Juwayti, and others.[4] The Mahdi's conquests in the early 1880s spelled the collapse of these particular houses, at least in the Sudan, but not the end of Syrian interests in that country. Upon the Anglo-Egyptian reconquest, they once again found a niche in the trade.[5] Thus 'Abdallah al-Kahhal's arrival in the Sudan may be seen as part of the larger Syrian penetration of the Nile Valley.[6]

His years in the Sudan are barely known. According to his grandson, Muhammad Mahmud 'Abdallah al-Kahhal, he married a Sudanese woman, although no children survived from the union.[7] After the defeat of General William Hicks Pasha and the conquest of El Obeid (January 1883), the capital of Kordofan province, 'Abdallah al-Kahhal was moved to approach the Mahdi to take the oath of allegiance. A valuable source of the period states that 'Abdallah al-Kahhal told the Mahdi about a "pious man in Jerusalem, of whom there was reason to hope that he would arise and call to God," that is to say, would become the Mahdi's follower. Upon learning this, the Mahdi wrote the Jerusalemite, summoning him to his cause and entrusting 'Abdallah al-Kahhal with carrying the message to Palestine.[8] 'Abdallah al-Kahhal, one would believe, used this as an excuse to leave the Sudan and departed via the unblocked western roads. He traveled through Darfur and Wadai and then turned northward to Libya. At various points he may have established contacts with authorities and merchants who later became useful to him. He came to Cairo sometime during the late 1880s or early 1890s and set up shop in Khan al-Khalili.[9] Egypt became his home until his death in 1921.

---

[4] Na'um Shuqayr, *Jughrâfiyyat wa târîkh as-Sûdân* (Beirut: Dâr al-Thaqâfa, 1967), 184–86.

[5] Ibid., 186.

[6] Thomas Philipp, *The Syrians in Egypt, 1725–1975* (Stuttgart: Steiner, 1985).

[7] Muhammad Mahmud 'Abdallah al-Kahhal, interview with the author, Cairo, October 11, 1971 (hereafter cited as Al-Kahhal Interview 1). The author expresses his gratitude to Muhammad al-Kahhal for his generosity of time and memories.

[8] Ismâ'l 'Abd al-Qâdir al-Kurdufani, *Sa'âdat al-mustahdî bi-sirât al-Imâm al-Mahdî*, trans. by Haim Shaked as *The Life of the Sudanese Mahdi* (New Brunswick, NJ: Transaction Books, 1978), 176. The letter was never found in the Mahdist archives (see al-Kurdufani, 176n181). According to Shuqayr (926), al-Kahhal was made *'amil* (agent, later commander) for Syria, which in the Mahdist vocabulary was the office directly below that of the *khalīfa*. Al-Kahhal's mission to Syria was therefore military. On the term, see P. M. Holt, *The Mahdist State in the Sudan, 1881–1898* (Oxford: Oxford University Press, 1958), 105–6.

[9] Shuqayr mentions that he came to Egypt via Wadai (926); his grandson suggests he also traveled to Darfur and Libya (Al-Kahhal Interview 1), which makes sense, considering

The British, the Western Sudan, and 'Abdallah al-Kahhal

The occupation of Egypt committed the British to the eventual overthrow of the Mahdiyya once the British position in Egypt was secured. However, as a Christian power in a Muslim sea they treaded carefully with Islamic religious movements and were eager to keep abreast of any internal situation that might be affected by Mahdist propaganda or by the Sanusiyya, whose headquarters lay near Egypt's western frontier. An Intelligence Department (ID) within the War Ministry was created in 1888 with Reginald Wingate as director. His duties were to "constantly oppose" Mahdists' interests in the Sudan, along Egyptian frontiers and within Egypt proper, in that order.[10] Agents were recruited to interview both foreigners resident in Egypt who had Sudan ties as well as travelers from the Sudan and the West. Intelligence diaries were compiled, and letters intercepted. Wingate was also convinced that the "future of the Egyptian Sudan would be affected by events in western Sudan"[11]—that is, in the kingdoms of Bornu, Bagirmi, and Wadai that as yet remained independent of European influence—and the ID kept careful track of pilgrims and merchants arriving from the West with news of those countries.

The career of Rabih ibn Fadlallah, sometimes called Rabih Zubayr, absorbed their interest on a number of counts. Once associated with Zubayr Rahma Mansur, whose clash with Charles George Gordon, later governor general of the Sudan, is well known and who was brought to Cairo and placed under house arrest, Rabih had broken away from the Mahdists and marched westward, conquering the southern provinces of Wadai and moving into the kingdom of Baghirmi. The kingdoms of Wadai and Bornu, as well as the Sokoto caliphate, were threatened. The British had little news of these developments, though their settlements in Nigeria lay closer to Rabih's field of action than did Egypt. When in 1893 a pilgrim arrived in

---

the trade routes. According to G. J. Lethem, whose information would have come from al-Kahhal's son, Mahmud, he was "long resident in Abeshe," the capital of Wadai: see Lethem to Palmer, August 4, 1925, Rhodes House (Bodleian Library), Oxford, Lethem Papers 11/1/fol. 72. I am grateful to the Bodleian Library, Oxford for giving me access to these papers.

[10] Reports compiled by the Egyptian Military Intelligence, now in a group known as CAIRINT stored in the National Records Office (hereafter NRO), Khartoum, Sudan, CAIRINT 1/30/161, "List of Secret Agents," dated 1893. The documents were stored via class, box, and folder.

[11] NRO, CAIRINT 3/18/300, "Memorandum on the Western Sudan," June 5, 1893.

Cairo from Kano bearing a letter from Rabih Zubayr to Zubayr Rahma Mansur—the "first written communication between Rabeh Zubair and Egypt for the space of 18 years," Wingate commented in a memo[12]—the British became aware of the possibilities of using Zubayr Rahma's influence to their advantage and of the communications network linking Cairo with Central Africa. Agents had already been reporting "arrivals" at Kirdasa from Libya and Wadai and of routes connecting Benghazi with Jalu oasis and Bornu. Although the chronology is fuzzy, it seems that at this time they entrusted a letter from Zubayr to Rabih with Muhammad Yunus, a Majbari trader, who succeeded only in getting as far as Jalu before the letter was confiscated by the Ottoman authority.[13] In their research for further news and other couriers, intelligence sources must have come across 'Abdallah al-Kahhal whom they discovered to be regularly corresponding with the head of the Sanusi order and with Majbari business associated in Benghazi and Jalu.

For example, Salim al-Mutawi, a Benghazi merchant, wrote him in December 1894 with news of Rabih's victories in Bornu. The letter appears in the monthly "Intelligence Report, Egypt," sure evidence that 'Abdallah al-Kahhal had by this time settled into an association with British intelligence officers. The letter may be quoted at length to show the type of information he was accustomed to receive:[14]

> Your letter dated 3rd November 1894,[15] to hand. Re the conquest of Bornu by Rabeh, merchants who had penetrated as far as the Bornu frontier, together with some of Rabeh's men, arrived yesterday from Wadai, and reported that Rabeh had taken possession of the Shenagra territories, south-west of Wadai, and also of the western provinces belonging to the Sultan.
>
> Last year Rabeh advanced on Baghirmi and besieged it for three months. The Sultan of Wadai sent a force to meet him, but it was defeated and retired. After a lapse of three months, Rabeh entered, and took the capital

[12] NRO, CAIRINT 3/18/300, "Memo on the Western Sudan," March 5, 1893.

[13] "Tales of the Wadai Slave Trade in the Nineties told by Yunes Bedis of the Majabra to W. E. Jennings Bramley," *Sudan Notes and Records* 23 (1940): 179–80.

[14] Letter from Salim al-Mutawi to 'Abdallah al-Kahhal, December 5, 1894, Benghazi, NRO, "Intelligence Report, Egypt" (hereafter IRE), no. 33, app. A. An almost complete set of these reports is also found in the Library of the War Office, London.

[15] Al-Kahhal could not write and used a scribe (Al-Kahhal Interview 1).

> of Baghirmi, and also the Sultan's harem and children, the Sultan withdrawing to a mountain called "Iri." Rabeh continued raiding the western provinces until met by the Bornu army, of 60,000 strong, under Emir Omar; a fierce battle was fought with great loss, the Bornu army eventually being put to flight. The Sultan fled towards Zender, but died on the road.
>
> Some of the Tripoli and Magharba Arab merchants who had accompanied the Bornu army returned to Bornu, others fled to Kano, about 12 days' journey from Bornu.
>
> These merchants were afraid of Rabeh, as they had formerly fought with the Bornu army; but eventually, after having collected 6,000 dollars, they bought themselves as a present to Rabeh, and begged for mercy. At first, Rabeh refused, but afterwards allowed them to return to their own homes, saying that, as the Fezzan road was not safe, he would send them by the Wadai route. He sent with them one of his Emirs with a valuable present for the Sultan, in the hope that this would induce him to open the road for trade. The Sultan refused the present, and Rabeh was obliged to send the merchants by a road through another country.
>
> The present consisted of 700 slaves, 50 loads of ivory, 10 kantars of feathers, 500 pieces of cloth.
>
> Rabeh meanwhile took possession of the capital, and the whole of the Shenagra country is now under his power.

The following spring and summer (1895) al-Mutawi wrote four letters to Zubayr, giving him news of Rabih as it was reported by sources in Benghazi. As Zubayr was under house arrest, all his letters were turned over to the Intelligence Department.[16] Then in May 1896, al-Hajj 'Urfan 'Abdallah, who had been in Kukuwa, the capital of Bornu, when Rabih's forces took the town, visited Cairo and sought Zubayr in the hope of obtaining a letter from him asking Rabih to return the property he had confiscated from 'Urfan 'Abdallah. Zubayr gave him the letter "with hesitation," but also gave him a letter to forward to Rabih that had been composed on the advice of the ID.[17] The response was not forthcoming for more than a year,

---

16 NRO, IRE, no. 38, 9–12; no. 39, 9,10; no. 40, 6–7.

17 NRO, CAIRINT 1/44/260, May 26, 1896.

and when it came, it was included in a letter from 'Urfan to 'Abdallah al-Kahhal, who had evidently been au courant of the matter.

"I went to see Kahhal yesterday," wrote Na'um Shuqayr, then a sub-director of ID, on September 25, 1897, "and he gave me a letter dated 17th Rabih Awal 1315 which he received from Hajj 'Urfan in Tripoli." The news was that Rabih would have "nothing to do with Zubeir," and he asked al-Kahhal "to show this letter to Shakoor Bey and then to Zubeir Pasha."[18] Further details of Rabih's letter would be forwarded when the messenger carrying the letter arrived in Tripoli.[19]

Shuqayr's meeting with 'Abdallah al-Kahhal seemed to have resulted in a new appreciation of the merchant's position and valuable contacts. Al-Kahhal told him, for example, that the head of the Sanusi lodge in Mecca was visiting Cairo en route to Kufra. Shuqayr noted in his report, "Kahhal seems to be in continual communication with the Shaikh Senussi. I saw in his shop two large books: the history of Ibn Athir and the history of Ibn Khaldun, which he tells me he is sending to Shaikh Senussi at Kufra." Shuqayr must have wondered at al-Kahhal's willingness to be so frank with him and his colleagues and could not have been surprised when he told him the suspicions his association was provoking. "Kahhal gives these news freely but he seems to be annoyed of Hassan bey Madkur who calls him a 'spy of the Intelligence.' He will come to see about all this," he added enigmatically.[20] But al-Kahhal's motives continued to arouse suspicion.

Sanusi Wakil in Cairo

The conquest of the Sudan preoccupied the ID from roughly 1897 to 1901, and during this period news of the western Sudan was played down. Once the Sudan was reopened, 'Abdallah al-Kahhal visited in early 1901. Along with other Egyptian and Syrian merchants, he reestablished his business

[18] At that time, Na'um Shuqayr was the Arabic secretary to the sirdar and later assistant director of military intelligence during the campaign for the recovery of the Sudan. See Richard Hill, *A Biographical Dictionary of the Sudan,* 2d ed. (London: Frank Cass and Co., 1967), 239.

[19] NRO, IRE, no. 49, app. X, letter dated July 26, 1896, Tripoli.

[20] NRO, CAIRINT 1/40/246, "Information re Rabeh, Senussi and Waddai," September 25, 1897.

ties, entrusting his affairs in Omdurman with an agent.[21] At this time he was also trading with Darfur, which regained its independence following the defeat of the Mahdiya, retaining Muhammad Anis as his agent there. He must have made the acquaintance of the famous old Darfur merchant Khabir Ali Ibrahim who was living there—if he did not meet him earlier in Sudan or Egypt—who later sought ‘Abdallah's help in persuading the British to expedite his request to return to al-Fashir where he had extensive properties.[22]

While in Omdurman, he received several letters from his son Mahmud that contained news he evidently thought significant. He approached H. H. S. Morant, a British soldier working in the Egyptian army and serving as an intelligence officer, who apparently did not know who he was. In his March report he wrote, “A certain merchant named Hajj Abdallah Kahhal brought letters . . . from his son in Cairo, giving the following information about affairs in Wadai, obtained from a certain Farhat Hassib, the Kadi of Jalo, who was on his way to Mecca.”[23] ‘Abdallah al-Kahhal was not a paid agent of the Intelligence Department and was under no obligation to report to its agents, so his approach in Omdurman requires an explanation. The news he had to disclose concerned the civil war that had broken out in Wadai and possible French intervention. It would appear that he had gone to the intelligence office in Omdurman to express his concern about the threat against the continued independence of the Wadai sultans and what seemed to be a developing collision between the Sanusis and the French.[24] The Wadai sultans being members of the Sanusi order, the “mother lodge” in Libya, would surely take measures to assist them.[25]

‘Abdallah Al-Kahhal returned to Cairo in May where he busied himself with Sanusi matters. He had become the Sanusi *wakil* (general agent) and for the next dozen years acted as their spokesman in Egypt. The author of a “History of Senussism” that appears in Intelligence Department files states that he “acted as agent for the Senussists in purchasing their

[21] On his agents, see sources in n. 78 (below).

[22] Reference to Muhammad Anis is found in NRO, Sudan Intelligence Reports (hereafter SIR), no. 80, app. E, 11; on Khabir Ali, see G. Michael La Rue, *Khabir Ali at Home in Kubayh: A Brief Biography of a Dar Fur Caravan Leader* (Boston: Boston University African Studies Center Working Papers, 1984), 15.

[23] SIR, no. 80, 2. On Morant, see Hill, *Biographical Dictionary,* 241.

[24] Cordell, 30–31.

[25] SIR, no. 133 (August 1905), report that the Sudanese were asking their brethren to converge on Wadai.

necessaries, clothing, building materials, etc., and in printing their books of history and prayer."[26] These tasks were sometimes rather petty. Once 'Abdallah al-Kahhal was sent some sword sheaths to have repaired.[27]

In becoming the Sanusi *wakil,* he also became the agent in Cairo of the Majabra, some of whom achieve high positions in the Sanusi order and a certain notoriety as travelers. Among 'Abdallah al-Kahhal's associates and correspondents were 'Abdallah al-Bishari and his family, Hamida Abu Dajaja, Muhammad Tahir Abu Safita, Muhammad "Baydis" Yunus, and Muhammad Fatita—most of whom were admired by Britons who met them in Egypt as much for their stamina and daring in long-distance travel as for their political awareness. Thomas Russell Pasha, who was Cairo chief of police, devotes five pages of his autobiography to a sketch of the al-Bishari family.[28] As he passed one of the Majabra caravans on his way to Siwa, Belgrave compared it to passing one of the famous trans-Atlantic ships on the open seas.[29]

In carrying out his duties as the Sanusi agent, 'Abdallah al-Kahhal succeeded in alienating neither the Sanusi leaders nor the British authorities although tensions could be expected to arise on both sides. There was, for instance, the affair of the tents. Na'um Shuqayr got whiff in May 1901 of the news that the Sanusis had placed an order for tents with 'Abdallah al-Kahhal. Rumors were circulating in Cairo that the Sanusi chief, Muhammad al-Mahdi, was planning to make the pilgrimage and would come from Kufra via the Darb al-Arba'in, passing through provincial cities in Upper Egypt at a time when anti-Christian sentiment was high. It would have created "some slight alarm in Egypt," one British official sanguincly put it,[30] and the ID was anxious to know whether there was any truth in the

---

[26] NRO, CAIRINT 2/15/125, "History of Senussism," October 25, 1905, probably prepared by Shuqayr. Muhammad al-Kahhal firmly denied that his grandfather exported books. This would have been done by the Halabi brothers, one of whom, 'Isa al-Babi al-Halabi, was married to 'Abdallah al-Kahhal's daughter, Amina. The Halabis were famous in the 1920s for their editions of books distributed widely in West Africa (G. J. F. Tomlinson and G. J. Lethem, *History of Islamic Propaganda in Nigeria* [London, 1927], 34), and the firm remained prominent in this trade until recently.

[27] NRO, CAIRINT 2/15/125, May 20, 1905.

[28] Thomas Russell, *Egyptian Service, 1902–1946* (London, 1949), 172–177.

[29] C. Dalrymple Belgrave, *Siwa: The Oasis of Jupiter Ammon* (London, 1923), 56.

[30] G. T. Forestier-Walker, "Notes on the History of Senussism and its Relations to the African Possessions of European Powers, Part I," prepared for the General Staff of the War Office, London, 1906, NRO, CAIRINT 2/15/125, 6.

rumor. Shuqayr visited al-Kahhal on May 13 to find out, but his denials of the rumor were apparently evasive. On May 20, Shuqayr reported in an irritated tone, "I sent for Kahhal yesterday and insisted upon him telling me the truth." 'Abdallah al-Kahhal replied that two tents "of the umbrella pattern" had already been dispatched with 'Abdallah al-Bishari, and that three years previously he had sent similar tents to the Sanusis, implying there was at that time no cause for alarm. He supposed they would be used for personal reasons and not employed in a pilgrimage. Shuqayr went on in his report, "On asking Kahhal why did he keep this secret from me before, he did not give a satisfactory answer, but I take it he heard we would seize the tents if we know [*sic*] about them and therefore he kept his secret until the tents are gone [*sic*]."[31] But Shuqayr believed in 'Abdallah al-Kahhal's basic trustworthiness, and there are no further words of suspicion in later reports.

Meanwhile 'Abdallah al-Kahhal was being assailed by the Sanusis in Egypt. He had doubtless heard the stories being circulated by Shaykh 'Abdallah Shitiwi, the erstwhile Sanusi agent in Cairo,[32] and must have been annoyed when he learned they had reached Benghazi as well. Al-Hajj Muhammad Fatita, one of his business associates and a confidant of the sultan of Wadai,[33] wrote him in June 1901, "I have been informed that Shteiwi says that El Kahhal and Feteita have sold Wadai to the English. You cannot revenge yourself, but let God take revenge from him in so much for all that he says."[34] Some years later al-Kahhal was visited by A. C. Parker of the ID and was still suffering from the effect of Shitiwi's slanders. He told Parker that Shitiwi was "a poor Maghrabi who studies at al-Azhar whence he receives a dole" and that he had been dismissed as the Sanusi agent in 1899, as Parker reported it,

> "for telling stories to the Khedive and receiving money from the Khedive's household. Even now he carries tales to a Eunuch of the Harem who tells them in the Palace and thus they come to the Khedive's ears, such tales being false stories of the Senussi's intentions and accusations against himself."[35]

---

[31] NRO, CAIRINT 2/15/125, May 20, 1901.

[32] NRO, CAIRINT 1/40/246, "Siwa and the Movement of the Senussi," report dated 1895.

[33] "Tales of the Wadai Slave Trade," 178; NRO, CAIRINT 2/15/125, report dated 1895.

[34] NRO, CAIRINT 2/15/125, letter dated June 8, 1901.

[35] NRO, CAIRINT 2/15/127, June 16, 1906.

But in 1901 he was concerned about compromising his position vis-à-vis the British, and when Shuqayr expressed a desire to interview 'Ali Kurjayli, one of the top Sanusi lieutenants, who was then visiting Cairo, he advised him against doing so.[36]

In June 'Abdallah al-Kahhal informed the ID of the death of Sultan Ibrahim of Wadai in fighting with his *'aqid*s (military commanders). His source was Muhammad al-Mahdi al-Sanusi, who relayed the development in a letter to the merchants of Benghazi.[37] About this time he sent 4,000 tins of gunpowder to the Sanusi headquarters, calming British fears by stating that the Sanusis planned no move toward Wadai or Darfur at this time.[38] He also reported that the French were claiming Wadai as part of their zone of influence while the British, if they wished, could move into Bornu.[39]

The British, meanwhile, were increasingly concerned about the Sanusi movements, fearing, among other things, that they would convert 'Ali Dinar, the sultan of Darfur, and move strategically into that kingdom,[40] thereby posing a menace to the still unsettled conditions in the Anglo-Egyptian Sudan. 'Abdallah al-Kahhal must have been pumped for information, but Lord Cromer, the British consul general in Egypt, also asked Consul Justin Alvarez in Benghazi to send him reports that he had.[41] The fear of pan-Islamism still figured heavily in British thinking, and it had a profound effect on British foreign policy in the Middle East as late as the beginning of World War I. Within the ID there were constant assessments of the possibility of a pan-Islamic jihad. In 1912 one Sudan-experienced analyst believed, however, that the Sanusi threat was exaggerated and offered the opinion that Sanusi warriors, while as good as the Ja'aliyyin, were not as skillful as the Hadendowa.[42]

---

36 NRO, CAIRINT 2/15/125, May 28, 1901. Kurjayli figures in several reports of fighting between the Sanusis and the French in 1908–9: see NRO, CAIRINT 2/15/128, March 23, 1908; January 31, 1909.

37 NRO, CAIRINT 2/15/125, June 5, 1901.

38 NRO, CAIRINT 2/15/125, anonymous note inscribed "Es-senousi," n.d. [June 20?] 1901; September 25, 1901.

39 NRO, CAIRINT 2/15/125, May 28, 1901.

40 NRO, CAIRINT 2/15/125, September 25, 1901; February 15, 1902: report that Abu Bakr al-Ghadamsi was heading a Sanusi mission to Darfur's capital, al-Fashir.

41 NRO, CAIRINT 2/15/125, April 24, 1902: report by Consul Alvarez pursuant to Lord Cromer's request.

42 PRO, WO106/214, "Report on the Western Desert," signed by V. Irwin, October 5, 1912, 4. On the pan-Islamic fears during this period and the international intrigue it inspired, see Donald McKale, "'The Kaiser's Spy': Max von Oppenheim and the Anglo-German

The Italians also used 'Abdallah al-Kahhal in an attempt to enhance their relations with the Sanusis. In 1903 the Cairo consulate's "Oriental Secretary," Muhammad 'Ali 'Alwi, asked 'Abdallah al-Kahhal to dispatch gifts to the Sanusi chief. He ordered a velvet saddle embroidered in silver, a pistol, a sword (engraved with the Sanusi's name), burnooses, and silk cloths, giving him a £50 advance on the cost of these purchases. 'Abdallah al-Kahhal forwarded this request to the ID and volunteered to ignore it if the ID disapproved,[43] but the department chiefs agreed, and the gifts were sent. Further correspondence was exchanged, as 'Abdallah al-Kahhal reported it, and another gift, this time rugs and calicoes, was sent with a Sanusi messenger.[44]

But 'Abdallah al-Kahhal proved to be anti-Italian, and when newspapers reporters came to him in 1908 asking if it were true that the Sanusis were receiving gifts from the Italian consulate, he told them it was not so. Then he wrote to the Sanusi head, saying "receiving presents from Europeans will lower him in the eyes of the Moslems" and advised him to refuse the gifts. He predicted to the ID "in all probability he will refuse to accept them."[45] But he was wrong. The Sanusi chief defended his friendship with "Said Ali Alwi" on the grounds it had "no worldly object. . . . He is a sherif and a follower of our sect. He is attached to us and wishes to keep in friendly communication with us."[46]

Muhammad al-Mahdi al-Sanusi died in 1903. Al-Kahhal supervised the construction of the cupola for the leader's tomb and had it shipped from Cairo. As described several years later, "A wooden cupola was made in Cairo through Hajj Abdalla al Kahhal to be erected over his shrine. It was made of thick and strong lata wood, plaited with brass of iron and crowned

---

Rivalry Before and During the First World War," *European History Quarterly* 27, no. 2 (1997): 199–219.

[43] NRO, CAIRINT 2/15/125, January 10, 1903; "History of Senussism," October 28, 1905, 13.

[44] NRO, CAIRINT 2/15/128, March 14, 1906; NRO, CAIRINT 2/15/125, "History of Senussism," October 28, 1905, 13 (mention of letter received in 1905). On Muhammad 'Ali 'Alwi, see Knut S. Vikor, *Sufi and Scholar on the Desert Edge: Muhammad b. Ali al-Sanusi and His Brotherhood* (Evanston, Ill.: Northwestern University Press, 1995), 12. He calls 'Alwi an "honorary interpreter" at the consulate who pretended to be the head of the Sanusiyya lodge in Cairo; however, Vikor believes that the Sanusis had no agent in Cairo but used contacts in Upper Egypt.

[45] NRO, CAIRINT 2/15/127, February 22, 1908.

[46] NRO, CAIRINT 2/15/128, June 11, 1908.

by a yellow brass crescent. It is square of eight metres; the crescent is two metres high. It left Cairo via Siwa in 1903."[47]

The remuneration 'Abdallah al-Kahhal received from the Sanusis for his various labors is not known. Intelligence sources noted that they sent him a black woman slave in 1906,[48] and his grandson says that he was given four slaves altogether.[49] Slavery was prohibited in Egypt from 1877, so the British authorities must have turned a blind eye to these gifts. Neither from this connection nor any other did 'Abdallah al-Kahhal amass a fortune.

Wadai and 'Abdallah al-Kahhal

Yusuf, the sultan of Wadai (1876–98), wrote in 1896 to "a well-known Cairo merchant"—a synonym in early intelligence reports for 'Abdallah al-Kahhal—urging him to "do his best to open a trade route between Wadai and Egypt."[50] It is the first documentary source we have on 'Abdallah al-Kahhal's relations with the sultanate, a relationship that he personally nurtured throughout the years he lived in Cairo.

There was a well-established route linking Wadai with Egypt before this time, via Libya and the Egyptian oases, which had been particularly strong from the 1860s onward. The sultan's plea can only be understood in light of the blockade of the Egyptian Sudan and the cessation of trade along the Darb al-Arba'in that had traditionally been used as a route for Wadai goods. Merchants and pilgrims were still reaching Cairo via the "western" route in the early 1890s, as reported in intelligence sources.[51]

As indicated earlier 'Abdallah al-Kahhal concerned himself personally with the politics of this kingdom and was especially interested in its skirmishes with the French. He apparently feared the victory of French forces there and took every opportunity to bring their aggressive intentions to the

---

47 NRO, CAIRINT 2/15/125, "History of Senussism," 5.

48 NRO, CAIRINT 2/15/128, January 14, 1906.

49 Muhammad Mahmud 'Abdallah al-Kahhal, interview with the author, Cairo, March 26, 1972 (hereafter cited as Al-Kahhal Interview 3): three of the women were named Hawa, Halima, and Bahr al-Zayn. They were buried in the al-Kahhal plot in the Mujawarin Cemetery, Cairo.

50 NRO, IRE No. 50 (from April 28, 1896 to December 31,1896), app. O.

51 NRO, IRE no. 21 (December 1893), 3; no. 27 (June 1894), 5; no. 37 (April 1895), 6–9.

attention of the ID. In 1901 he warned of possible French intervention in the civil war between Yusuf's successor, Sultan Ibrahim, and the *'aqid*s.[52] Upon the death of Sultan Ibrahim in 1901, Muhammad Fatita suggested he send gifts to his successor,[53] and while it is not sure whether he did, in 1906 he is known to have sent a watch to the new sultan, named Muhammad "Dudmurra" Salih, that was engraved with his name.[54] In 1902 he turned over letters containing fresh news from Wadai from correspondents in Libya who reported the approach of French forces;[55] and in 1904 he turned over another report of renewed fighting between the French and the sultan of Baghirmi.[56] By this time, he had become Dudmurra's agent in Cairo, forwarding goods to him as requested, including, perhaps, arms.[57] In this capacity he was also known to French military and diplomatic sources that viewed his activities with suspicion.[58]

As agent, 'Abdallah al-Kahhal also carried out some of the sultan's benefactions. He received a letter from Dudmurra in 1908, for instance, informing him that 16 qantars of ivory were being shipped to Benghazi, the proceeds of which sale were to be distributed among designated religious and charitable institutions in Egypt and the Hejaz. He also sent two eunuchs to be delivered to the Holy Cities. The ivory was sold for £570 by Muhammad Abu Dajaja in Benghazi and the money was duly forwarded to Cairo. Of the total, four-fifths of the proceeds were earmarked for employees at the mosques of Mecca and Medina and to other persons and places

---

52 NRO, CAIRINT 2/15/125, April 24, 1901. On French and Turkish movements in northern Wadai and in the central Sahara at this time, Knut S. Vikor, *"An Episode of Saharan Rivalry: The French Occupation of Kawar, 1906," International Journal of African Historical Studies* 18 (1985): 699–715.

53 NRO, CAIRINT 2/15/125, letter dated June 8, 1901.

54 NRO, CAIRINT 2/15/128, January 18, 1906.

55 NRO, CAIRINT 2/15/127, October 11, 1903.

56 NRO, CAIRINT 2/15/127, February 25, 1904.

57 NRO, CAIRINT 2/15/125, August 20, 1907. The extent to which 'Abdallah al-Kahhal was involved in arms trading is not known. It was against the law, but according to numerous intelligence reports, arms were being exported almost on a regular basis from Cairo and Alexandria. Al-Kahhal did send 4,000 "tins" of gunpowder to the Sanusis in1901 (NRO, CAIRINT 2/15/125, September 25, 1901) and admitted at the time that 7,000 "old fashioned rifles" had in the last year been smuggled out of Cairo to the Sanusis. But he himself was too close to the British authorities to engage in this trade.

58 Commandant Henri Gadens, "Les états musulmans de l'Afrique Centrale et leurs rapports avec La Mecque et Constantinople," *Questions diplomatiques et coloniales* 24 (1907): 445.

in the Holy Cities (many of whom would have been eunuchs), while the remainder, approximately £125, went to students from Wadai, Darfur, and Sinnar (at al-Azhar University), as well as to the Cairo mosques of Imam Ahmad al-Badawi (Tanta), Ibrahim al-Dusuqqi (Dussuq), and Imam al-Shafi'i, and to a mosque called "Imam Narma."[59]

Fearing collusion amongst the pan-Islamists, the British sent this information to Consul Alvarez for comment. In his view, he thought the donations had been made "at Senussi instigation, especially those . . . to the servants of the 'Haram Sherif,'" but concluded vacuously, "It is perhaps premature at present to state what political object the Sultan of Wadai has in view of the connection with his evident desire to stand well with the people of influence in the Holy Places and elsewhere unless he intends to go on pilgrimage."[60] Al-Kahhal left shortly thereafter for the Hejaz to carry out the sultan's wishes.

But 'Abdallah al-Kahhal was himself attentive to the welfare of Wadai pilgrims in Cairo. Those who could not afford to stay in hotels or lacked friends in the city were often invited to lodge in the Wakalat al-Kahhal, which was located near al-Azhar Mosque. Al-Kahhal's grandson Muhammad remembers seeing as a boy pilgrims sleeping and eating while they stayed in the caravansary.[61]

'Abdallah al-Kahhal became increasingly confident in his unofficial diplomatic role. He concerned himself with the continuing bad relations between Wadai and neighboring Darfur, which had led to a "war" during 1902–4 and to severely strained ties in 1906. Muhammad al-Bishari, who arrived from Wadai in February 1906 and saw 'Abdallah al-Kahhal almost daily, reported that the sultan was imprisoning any Wadaian who went to Darfur.[62] In June 'Abdallah al-Kahhal passed on information that the *'aqid* of Mahamid had attacked a Darfur force and defeated it.[63] About this time, he wrote Sultan 'Ali Dinar of Darfur—without the knowledge of the ID—a letter of general advice in which he urged the sultan to come to terms with the Anglo-Egyptian government or else "take immediate steps to establish peace between yourself and the sultan of Wadai, so that in case

---

[59] NRO, CAIRINT 2/15/128, December 1, 1908.

[60] NRO, CAIRINT 2/15/128, Alvarez to Various, Tripoli, Libya, December 16, 1908.

[61] Al-Kahhal Interview 1.

[62] NRO, CAIRINT 2/15/128, February 28, 1906.

[63] NRO, CAIRINT 2/15/128, June 16, 1906, contradicting an earlier report on March 3, 1906.

of defeat you will find some power with whom you can take refuge."[64] Peace was a long time in coming, but when it did, according to reports reaching Cairo in February 1908, 'Abdallah al-Kahhal modestly claimed some of the credit.[65]

The French now moved determinedly on Wadai. The fall of Abeche on June 2, 1909, was reported in a letter to 'Abdallah al-Kahhal by Hamida Abu Dajaja from Benghazi on August 11, and by a brother of the *qâdî* of Abeche on August 31.[66] Sultan Dudmurra was reported to have fled to al-Dur, but without his troops.[67] Deeply concerned, 'Abdallah al-Kahhal petitioned the French government to allow the sultan to leave and to grant him a pension on condition that he reside in Egypt or the Sudan. According to an ID source, he was "sanguine as to the result of these proposals and has informed the Senussi of his action."[68] Al-Kahhal's letter was forwarded to the governor-general of the French Congo and then to the lieutenant governor of Oubangui-Chari-Tchad—in other words, into bureaucratic oblivion, and it was apparently never acted upon.[69]

A delegation from the French-installed sultan arrived in Omdurman in 1911 with the object of purchasing goods and visiting the Sudan before proceeding north to Cairo to see 'Abdallah al-Kahhal.[70] There is no further word of their meeting. It seems highly unlikely, however, that after the French conquest 'Abdallah al-Kahhal could have been of much use to the sultans, and in any event his services would have encountered strong resistance from the French.

'Abdallah al-Kahhal's Trade

When asked what qualities were necessary to operate in the long-distance trade in camels, Abu'l-Qasim 'Ali Ahmed, the venerable chief of the camel market outside Cairo, once told me "contacts in the Sudan and money."[71]

---

[64] NRO, CAIRINT 2/15/128, February 12, 1908. His explanation to the ID was that he hoped his advice would please both Darfur, Wadai, and the Sanusis, and that he was also "looking only to the prosperity of his trade in both places."

[65] NRO, CAIRINT 2/15/128, February 12, 1908.

[66] NRO, CAIRINT 2/15/128, August 11, 1901.

[67] NRO, CAIRINT 2/15/129, December 27, 1909.

[68] NRO, SIR, no. 185 (December 1909), 7.

[69] NRO, CAIRINT 2/15/128, December 12, 1909.

[70] NRO, SIR, no. 204 (July 1911), 5.

[71] Abu'l-Qasim 'Ali Ahmed, interview with the author, at the Cairo camel market in Barajil, April 1971.

This rule of thumb might also have applied to merchants such as 'Abdallah al-Kahhal in the late nineteenth century. It also required faith and patience, for returns on investments were both slow and impossible to guarantee.

'Abdallah al-Kahhal bought ivory feathers, skins, and gum from long-distance merchants (*jallaba*) and sold cloth, beads, scents, and guns (though the last was illegal).[72] He did not deal in camels, an important component of the trade. "Send me the price of camels," Muhammad Abu Safita wrote in 1904, having no doubt heard of the cattle plague that was raging in Egypt.[73] Later, as trade opened up with the Sudan again, he dealt in pepper, white beans, butter, sesame seed, and *karkaday* (hibiscus leaves). Of textiles, he specialized in cheap *kham* cottons that circulated in the Sudan under the trade name Dammur, as well as in *hijazi* sheets "in bright colors" that were made in Cairo, in *fuwat* (kerchiefs) with yellow-and-black stripes on brick-red, in *dablan* (known in Egypt as *maqsura,* which was a coarse Manchester-made cloth that was usually dyed in Cairo), and in a variety of ready-made items—trousers, burnooses, drawers, vests, and *jallabiya*s (robes for men).[74] The 1905 edition of *Dalil Masr wa Sudan,* a commercial who's who among traders and merchants, lists 'Abdallah al-Kahhal as a rug merchant.[75] Eventually the family business became entirely concerned with rugs.

His grandson recalled that 'Abdallah al-Kahhal took a percentage on goods he sold for merchants and occasional travelers.[76] In Cairo he had no business associates, but in the Sudan and Libya he used a variety of agents. His Benghazi partner after 1906 was Hamida Abu Dajaja, a contact well placed in the Sudan trade as he had spent eight years in Wadai.[77] His agents in Omdurman were mostly Syrians who had come to Egypt without work who formed partnerships with 'Abdallah al-Kahhal, and with the capital

[72] Al-Kahhal Interview 1.

[73] NRO, CAIRINT 2/15/127, February 25, 1904; see also the report dated May 8, 1904. The Abu Safita family were originally from the Fezzan (Libya) and were prominent in al-Fashir in later years as agents of the trade of Darfur: see the note by R. S. O'Fahey on the family, made available on the Internet by the Center for Middle Eastern Studies, University of Bergen: http://64.233.169.104/search?q=cache:X9_2JvD710kJ:www.smi.uib.no/darfur/NOTES%2520from%2520NRO.doc+%22abu+safita%22&hl=en&ct=clnk&cd=1&gl=us.html (accessed May 14, 2008).

[74] Al-Kahhal Interviews 1 and 3; Muhammad Mahmud 'Abdallah al-Kahhal, interview with the author, Cairo, November 12, 1971 (hereafter Interview 2); "Tales of the Wadai Slave Trade," 171.

[75] *Dalil Masr wa Sudan* (Sudan, 1905), 186.

[76] Al-Kahhal Interview 1.

[77] NRO, CAIRINT 2/15/128, July 25, 1906; February 11, 1908.

he advanced—usually £100–£200—they were usually able to gain entry permits from the British and settle in the Sudan. According to his grandson, al-Kahhal realized little, if no, return on these ventures.[78]

The Wakalat al-Kahhal on Sharia Bedistan was owned by Amir Sayf al-Din and was a typical caravansary structure. It had two stories with shops or storerooms on the ground floor and a *rab'* (living accommodations) on the second level. A large open courtyard was in the center. Of the ten storerooms, for which the occupants paid no more than 50 piastres a month in rent, al-Kahhal occupied five in addition to an "office" opposite the doorway. In later years, other storerooms were occupied by Ahmad Ahmad Abu Sa'ud, a Cairene, and Ibrahim Zayn, a Sudanese, both of whom also dealt in Sudan goods. The Abu Sa'uds—Ahmad and his brother Muhammad—eventually established a shop in Kano where they flourished from 1929–39;[79] Ibrahim Zayn was recalled many years later as "one of the biggest of the Sudan merchants."[80]

'Abdallah al-Kahhal and the British

'Abdallah al-Kahhal was suspected of being pro-British by his enemies in Cairo. It would have been difficult to hide the visits of British Intelligence Department officers who appeared regularly in his shop. Once al-Kahhal even visited the home of Russell Pasha, the police chief.[81] While there is no doubt that he was in fact pro-British, it is also true to say that despite this predilection he retained the confidence of the Sanusis who at that time represented an anti-European Muslim movement.

What is more, the Sanusis probably also appreciated the respect 'Abdallah al-Kahhal had among well-placed British officials and sent him letters obviously to be shared by them. In 1911, for example, the Sanusi chief wrote at length about the difficulties with the French—"the more we avoid this French foe and go out of his way, the more he follows us and does us harm," he complained, and then he contrasted the French attitude unfavorably with the British:

---

[78] Al-Kahhal Interview 3. Agents recalled by name were 'Abd al-Qadir Tulaimat (see CAIRINT 2/15/129, October 27, 1912) and al-Hajj Nasir al-'Askar.

[79] Muhammad Ahmad Abu Sa'ud, interview with the author, Cairo, March 1972.

[80] Muhammad Zayn is mentioned by Shuqayr, 184; Ibrahim Zayn was remembered by in an interview with Abu'l-Qasim 'Ali Ahmad.

[81] Russell, 175.

> Take the English, who are our neighbors in Egypt. They have done us no harm, to our zawias or our brethren. On the contrary, they treat our places in Egypt and Kano with the greatest honor and respect. We ask God to insert Islam in their hearts and the love of its peoples, as there is an old traditional saying that sometime in the future the victory of the Muhammadan religion will be accomplished through their instrumentality.[82]

'Abdallah Al-Kahhal turned this letter over to the ID, but Lee Stack, then director, was unimpressed. He commented in a note, "As the original of the above letter has been seen, there is no doubt as to its authenticity. It is, however, in my opinion written expressly for local French and English consumption in Egypt and the Sudan."[83]

'Abdallah Al-Kahhal became *bab al-gharb* (spokesman for the West [i.e., North Africa]), as it was put some years later[84]—and for his willingness to confide in the British his unusually informed correspondence gave them access to information otherwise inaccessible. But he also kept abreast of news from Sudan, Syria, and Arabia, and, although he never returned to Damascus, he made frequent trips to the Holy Cities on behalf of the sultans of Wadai. He became friendly with the sharifs of Mecca and was acquainted from the beginning with the Arab Revolt. T. E. Lawrence consulted him about the general situation and asked his advice as to what gifts he should take to the sharifs. He spent much time supervising the making of these presents.[85]

The British threw business to him whenever they could. The Sudan Agency commissioned him to make gifts they distributed to tribal chiefs in the Sudan—trays, large drums, swords, robes of honor (worked with gold and silver threads and sometimes attached with medals).[86] During World War I, he was given the right to distribute export licenses for sugar and rice to Palestine and Syria. This was done without a fee being charged, and according to his grandson, al-Kahhal did not gain financially from this position. Philipp in his study of the Syrians in Egypt contrasts the Chris-

---

[82] NRO, CAIRINT 2/15/129, April 9, 1911.

[83] Ibid.

[84] Lethem to Palmer, August 4, 1925, Lethem Papers, 11/1/fol. 75, referring to 'Abdallah's son, Mahmud.

[85] Ronald Storrs, *Orientations* (London, 1937), 299; Al-Kahhal Interview 1, referring to the gifts.

[86] Al-Kahhal Interview 3. "Traded in robes of honor" is how Lethem viewed this activity: see Tomlinson and Lethem, 36.

tian and the Muslims in that community, pointing out that Christians developed an extensive European business under the British while Muslim Syrians did not.[87]

'Abdallah al-Kahhal is remembered in the memoirs of Sir James Rennell Rodd,[88] Russell Pasha, and Sir Ronald Storrs, but perhaps the most poignant remembrance of his friendships with these men is that recalled by his grandson, Muhammad al-Kahhal. He had the following story to tell:

> I met him [Storrs] only once. One day I was sitting in the office of the great Wakalat al-Kahhal and a large man entered the office with his hat drawn low on his head. Behind me was a picture of my grandfather, 'Abdallah al-Kahhal. He came into the room and looked at the picture and then took off his hat, bowed, and put it back on again. Then he turned to me and said, "Who are you?" I said, "Muhammad al-Kahhal, son of Mahmud." Storrs said, "And who is that man?" pointing to the picture. "That is 'Abdallah al-Kahhal, my grandfather." He then took my hand and introduced himself, saying he was an old friend of 'Abdallah's.[89]

Conclusion

The last two decades of the nineteenth century and first decade of the twentieth witnessed profound political turmoil in Northeast and Central Africa. The steady encroachment of Europe absorbed in piecemeal fashion this enormous region. Nevertheless, trade continued to flow through the Libyan corridor, the last to succumb to European imperialism, with much impediment. Egypt, although occupied by the British and effectively cut off from its former territories in the Sudan, benefited from its border with Libya and its trans-Saharan trade connections.

The full picture of Libyan trade with Egypt during this period is not complete. Egyptian foreign trade figures do not account for it; and, in any event, the gaps in existing records do not allow for a cumulative overview. The records of British customhouses, which have been used in the present

[87] Al-Kahhal Interview 3. This point could not be checked in British sources; see also Philipp.*The Syrians in Egypt, op.cit.*

[88] Sir James Rennell Rodd, *Social and Diplomatic Memoirs, 1894–1901* (London: E. Arnold, 1923), 74, in relating to a story about Blunt's visit to Siwa oasis.

[89] Muhammad Mahmud 'Abdallah al-Kahhal, interview with the author, Cairo, August 1976.

article, reflect only that portion absorbed by Britain. Imports of ivory, feathers, and gum may have come on the Egyptian market from Libya, or they may have been counted among goods transiting Egypt from the Red Sea ports. They make clear that during the period of the Mahdiya, the volume of trade in African goods fell to 15 percent of levels achieved earlier.

On the other hand, the correspondence of ʻAbdallah al-Kahhal—that part that has survived in the records of the British Intelligence Department—evidences a steady, active intercourse between Cairo merchants and the Sanusiya and, through their contacts, with northern Nigeria and Wadai. The heavy political content of ʻAbdallah al-Kahhal's letters should not obscure the reasons for their having been written. ʻAbdallah al-Kahhal was first and foremost a merchant. Gossip to the contrary, he did not earn a livelihood from an exchange of political news.

Whatever the letters show, they exhibit an extraordinary interest in the affairs of Africa: in the Sanusiya, the sultans of Wadai, the sultans of Darfur, and events in the Sudan and Nigeria. They are particularly valuable for what they tell us about the scope of Egyptian commercial concerns, be they in the political sphere, the welfare of pilgrims, or commodity prices. In the absence of similar documents from other Egyptian sources, they shed light on the links between Cairene merchants and their trading partners in trans-Saharan Africa, the type of links that existed in earlier periods.

THE *KĀSHIF AL-ILBĀS* OF SHAYKH IBRĀHĪM NIASSE: ANALYSIS OF THE TEXT

Zachary Wright

The *Kāshif al-Ilbās* was the magnum opus of one of twentieth-century West Africa's most influential Muslim leaders, Shaykh al-Islam Ibrāhīm 'Abd-Allāh Niasse (1900–1975). No Sufi master can be reduced to a single text, and the mass following of Shaykh Ibrāhīm, described as possibly the largest single Muslim movement in modern West Africa,[1] most certainly found its primary inspiration in the personal example and spiritual zeal of the Shaykh rather than in written words. The analysis of this highly significant West African Arabic text cannot escape the essential paradox of Sufi writing: putting the ineffable experience of God into words. The *Kāshif* repeatedly insisted that the communication of "experiential spiritual knowledge" (*ma'rifa*)—the key concept on which Shaykh Ibrāhīm's movement was predicated and the subject which occupies the largest portion of the

[1] Portions of this article are included in the introduction to the forthcoming publication: Zachary Wright, Muhtar Holland, and Abdullahi El-Okene, trans., *The Removal of Confusion Concerning the Flood of the Saintly Seal, Aḥmad al-Tijānī: A Translation of* Kāshif al-Ilbās 'an fayḍa al-khatm Abī al-'Abbās *by Shaykh al-Islam al-Ḥājj Ibrāhīm b. 'Abd-Allāh Niasse* (Louisville, Ky.: Fons Vitae, 2010). See Mervyn Hiskett, *The Development of Islam in West Africa* (London: Longman, 1984), 287. See also Ousmane Kane, John Hunwick, and Rüdiger Seesemann, "Senegambia I: The Niassene Tradition," in *The Writings of Western Sudanic Africa,* vol. 4 of *Arabic Literature of Africa,* ed. John Hunwick and R. S. O'Fahey, 272–307, 276 (Leiden: Brill, 2003), where the Shaykh is described: "Without a doubt, one of the greatest figures of Islam and the Tijāniyya in twentieth century Africa."

Islamic Africa, VOL. 1, NO. 1, 2010. ISSN 2154-0993. www.islamicafricajournal.org

Kāshif—was beyond words. The Shaykh wrote of spiritual experience or "taste" (*dhawq*):

> Know that this science we mention is not mere wagging of the tongue. Its contents are spiritual experiences (*adhwāq*) and ecstasy (*wijdān*). It cannot be acquired through talking or written texts, but can only be received directly from the people of experience (*ahl al-adhwāq*). It can only be gained through serving (*khidma*) the people of spiritual distinction (*rijāl*), and companionship with the perfected ones. By Allah, no one has ever succeeded (on this path) except by companionship with one who has succeeded, and the achievement is from Allah.[2]

Even if recent academic research has rightly devalued the role of texts in the transmission of Sufi knowledge,[3] none can deny the continued relevance of studying the writings of prominent Sufis. Moreover, serious textual consideration of West African Sufism has been stifled by lingering colonial prejudice of a supposedly distinct, synchronistic Islam Noir (Negro Islam) and by thinly veiled disdain for black African scholars.[4] Time

---

[2] Shaikh al-Islam Ibrāhīm 'Abd-Allāh Niasse, *Kāshif al-Ilbās 'an fayḍa al-khatm Abī al-'Abbās* (Cairo: Shaykh Tijānī Cisse, 2001), p. 45.

[3] Proceedings from "Sufi Texts, Sufi Contexts," a workshop held at the Institute for the Study of Islamic Thought in Africa (ISITA), Northwestern University, Evanston, Ill., May 28–29, 2007, particularly the presentations of Carl Ernst ("Sufi Literature and Its Reception in History"), Valerie Hoffman ("Concluding Remarks"), and Rüdiger Seesemann ("Three Ibrahims").

[4] An expert on French colonial knowledge of Islam, for example, said Shaykh Ibrāhīm's books "apparently lack originality" (J. C. Froelich, *Les Musulmans d'Afrique Noire* [Paris: Éditions de l'Orante, 1962], 236). A later Islamologist, Michel Chodkiewicz, concludes that Shaykh Ibrāhīm Niasse had no direct contact with the writings of Ibn al-'Arabī (d. 1240), one of Islam's greatest thinkers. This can only mean it was Chodkiewicz who never had direct contact with Shaykh Ibrāhīm's writings: the *Kāshif* is in fact replete with precise chapter references to Ibn al-'Arabī's greatest works. See Michel Chodkiewicz, *Ocean Without Shore: Ibn 'Arabî, the Book and the Law* (Albany: State University of New York Press, 1993), 10–11. A version of Chodkiewicz's introduction to *Ocean Without Shore* also appears separately as Michel Chodkiewicz, "The Diffusion of Ibn 'Arabi's Doctrine," *Journal of the Muhyiddin Ibn 'Arabi Society* 9 (1991), http://www.ibnarabisociety.org/articles/diffusion.html (accessed December 13, 2009). Chodkiewicz writes in this latter piece: "A dissident of the Tijâniyya, Ibrâhîm Nyass could assuredly find many elements of akbarian origin in the masters of this *tarîqa.* But I am led to believe that his eschatological beliefs owe a lot to the *Yawâqît* [of Sha'rānī], and very little (or more likely nothing) to an assiduous familiarity with the works of Ibn 'Arabi." It seems to have escaped Chodkiewicz that

and again, the received knowledge concerning African Muslims' lack of scholarly qualifications substitutes for actual study of their teachings and writings. West African Arabic writings deserve a closer look.

Shaykh Ibrahim's *Kāshif al-Ilbās* provides an illuminating window into the world of a twentieth-century West African Muslim scholar. The book is certainly informed by its historical context, but it tackles some of the most widespread debates in the Muslim world. The author was clearly immersed in a rich Muslim scholarly tradition spanning several centuries and continents. The sources cited demonstrate a profound familiarity with a range of specialties within the Islamic sciences. Moreover, the wholesale commitment to the necessity of "gnosis" (*ma'rifa*) for every sincere Muslim seems unprecedented—dare we say original—even if the author is careful to substantiate his claims with citations from previous works. Analysis of the *Kāshif* thus provides important evidence that West African Muslim scholarship in the early twentieth century was cosmopolitan, diverse and both innovative and deeply rooted in the Islamic tradition.

Understanding the contents of the *Kāshif al-Ilbās* requires some background of the life and mission of its author.[5] Shaykh Ibrāhīm was a Muslim scholar and sage of the Tijāniyya Sufi order. The Tijāniyya has spread to all corners of the Muslim world since Shaykh Aḥmad al-Tijānī (d. 1815, Fez) established the confraternity in North Africa in the late eighteenth century. Many eminent scholars have emerged among the Tijāniyya in the last two centuries, but few have been as successful in propagating the order as Shaykh Ibrāhīm. No external statistics for the number of those

---

the *Kāshif* contains frequent precise references to the works of Ibn al-'Arabī but only one reference to Sha'rānī's *Yawāqīt.* Indeed, Chodkiewicz's characterization of Niasse, whom he mistakenly labels as a "dissident" and elsewhere as "another black African Sufi," seems prejudiced from the start.

[5] For more information on the life and thought of Shaykh Ibrahim Niasse, see Rüdiger Seesemann, *Sufism in Context: Ibrahim Niasse and the Emergence of a 20th-Century West African Sufi Movement* (Oxford: Oxford University Press, forthcoming); Joseph Hill, "Divine Knowledge and Islamic Authority: Religious Specialization Among Disciples of Baay Ñas" (Ph.D. thesis, Yale University, 2007); Andre Brigaglia, "The *Fayda* Tijaniyya of Ibrahim Nyass: Genesis and Implications of a Sufi Doctrine," in *Islam et sociétés au sud du Sahara* (Paris: Éditions de la Maison des Sciences de l'Homme, 2001), 41–56, 14–15; Ousmane Kane, "Shaykh al-Islam al-Ḥājj Ibrahim Niasse," in *Le temps des Marabouts: Itinéraires et stratégies islamiques en Afrique occidentale française v. 1880–1960,* ed. David Robinson and Jean-Louis Triaud, 299–316 (Paris: Karthala, 2000); Mervyn Hiskett, "The Community of Grace and Its Opponents, the Rejecters," in *African Language Studies* (London: School of Oriental and African Studies, University of London, 1980), 99–140, 17n.

tracing their Tijānī affiliation through Shaykh Ibrāhīm are available, but internal estimates claim one hundred million followers, or more than half of all Tijānīs in the world.[6]

Shaykh Ibrāhīm explained his historical mission in spreading Islam and the Tijāniyya throughout West Africa and beyond as being endowed with Al-Fayḍat al-Tijāniyya, the "Tijānī Flood" predicted by Shaykh Aḥmad al-Tijānī that would occasion people entering the Tijānī spiritual path group upon group. If *fayḍa* was the doctrine, the distinguishing practice of Shaykh Ibrāhīm's movement was *tarbiya,* or "spiritual training." Through *tarbiya,* aspirants transcended the confines of their ego-selves and "tasted" the directly experienced knowledge, or "gnosis" (*ma'rifa*), of God. Certainly this practice was nothing new within Sufism or the Tijāniyya itself, but Shaykh Ibrāhīm's ability to help millions attain the highly valued "spiritual illumination" (*fatḥ*) was surely unprecedented. Of course, there is much more to the story of Shaykh Ibrāhīm—his adaptive legal rulings, his creation of a grassroots pan-African and pan-Islamic movement, his world travels and close relations with some of his day's most renowned revolutionary leaders (Kwame Nkrumah, Sekou Touré, and Gamal Abdel Nasser, for example)—but this concept of a flood of gnosis, spiritual illumination for all who desired it, was the key to understanding the Shaykh's life and mission.

The *Kāshif al-Ilbās,* written early on in the Shaykh's career in 1931–32, was primarily a justification for the transmission of the "experiential knowledge" (*ma'rifa*) of God on a widespread scale. The self's complete immersion and annihilation in the Divine Essence, which Sufism has long maintained is essential for true knowledge of God, is a concept that has been fraught with tension throughout Islamic history, both among the detractors of Sufism and among Sufis themselves. The aspirant who becomes "enraptured" in God may behave as one absent from his senses or he may make extraordinary spiritual claims. The *Kāshif* thus presented the means of attaining "gnosis" (*ma'rifa*) and the results of such knowledge for its possessor. In so doing, the work differentiated false pretensions from

---

[6] Statistics presented by Shaykh Hassan Cisse at the International Tijānī Forum in Fez, Morocco, June 28, 2007. Shaykh Hassan justified this figure by reference to his own extensive personal travel throughout Africa, discussion with local *muqaddam*s, and statistics claimed for specific countries on various African media outlets. For this latter, Shaykh Hassan referenced a recent radio broadcast in Nigeria positing the number of Shaykh Ibrāhīm's followers in Nigeria at forty million. Independent verification of such figures would require a separate study on its own.

sincere expression, delusion from real experience, and heretical claims from Islamic orthodoxy.

Shaykh Ibrāhīm's method in this regard was to urge the disciple's combination of "rapture" (*jadhb*) and "traveling the path" (*sulūk*). A few lines of the Shaykh's own poetry from the *Kāshif* illustrate this key point:

> O enraptured one! If you do not travel the difficulties of the path
> Alas for you, you are incomplete; so continue seeking
>
> O seeker! If you do not become enraptured
> You remain veiled, so move and bestir yourself!
>
> The perfected one is he who combines
> The two states of rapture and seeking, it is he who progresses with speed
>
> May Allah include us among such perfected ones
> Who have become truly enraptured, but continued traveling the path.[7]

As the key issue of the *Kāshif,* the issue of Divine gnosis, and the possibility of its mass transmission through the Tijānī *Fayḍa,* was certainly one of the currents in early twentieth-century West Africa. But it was not the only issue of dispute to which Shaykh Ibrāhīm was responding in his work. Around the time the *Kāshif* was written, there seems to have been a lively debate in Senegal over whether it was possible to "see" God. For followers of Shaykh Ibrāhīm, seeing God seems intimately connected to attaining *ma'rifa* in the process of *tarbiya.*[8] It is not a topic of *'aqīda,* or "theology." The fact that it became an issue of theological dispute over what constitutes proper belief or conceptualization of God's identity is itself evidence that gnosis was becoming widespread in the region at this time.

In any case, the debate would erupt in a series of polemical exchanges immediately after the *Kāshif*'s writing, between the followers of Shaykh Ibrāhīm and Aḥmad Dem (d. 1973), a Fulani scholar living in Sokone, Senegal.[9] Shaykh Ibrāhīm's position on this issue, to which he devoted an

---

[7] *Kāshif,* 118.

[8] I observed Shaykh Hassan Cisse ask a student beginning *tarbiya:* "Go find Allah, and come back and tell me what you see." Shaikh Hassan Cisse, in discussion with the author, Medina-Baye Kaolack, Senegal, December 2008.

[9] Aḥmad Dem's polemical work against the possibility of "seeing" God was entitled *Tanbīḥ al-Aghbiyā'.* It produced immediate refutations from 'Uthmān Ndiaye, whose work was entitled *Sawārim al-Ḥaqq,* and from 'Alī Cisse, whose work was entitled *Mikhzam li Abāṭil*

entire chapter in the *Kāshif,* was more nuanced than the ensuing polemical exchange would indicate:

> The substance of the issue is that the vision of Allah with the eyes, today in this world, is conceivable, even if it has not been legally demonstrated. As for the vision by means of spiritual insight (*baṣīra*), experience (*dhawq*), and unveiling (*kashf*), its occurrence is an indisputable fact. The expressions of the Sufi people differ concerning the vision of Allah. Some express it as not seeing any existence (*wujūd*) aside from the Real. Others say it means self-annihilation (*fanā'*), or others express it as the arrival in the Divine Presence (*wuṣūl*). Some say it means union with the Divine (*jam'*).[10]

His argument in this regard was consistent with his method elsewhere: the Shaykh took the time to address the question from a variety of perspectives. The chapter begins with a presentation of what scholars of jurisprudence and theology have said about the vision of God before providing testimony from the Sufi tradition as to real meaning of seeing God. He thus conceded certain difficulties if Sufi expressions should be limited to one perspective, such as a narrow legalistic framework, but reasserted the essential meaning of the concept. The result is a skillful defense of the Sufi experience of witnessing the Real, essentially making it palatable to a larger audience.

There are other important questions also addressed in the *Kāshif,* some of more limited historical scope, and others that still are of relevance to Muslims today. The emphasis on public recitation of Sufi litanies, for example, no doubt responds to the century-old dispute between scholars of the Tijānī and Qādirī Sufi orders in Northern Nigeria and elsewhere over whether Sufis should recite their liturgies silently or out loud in public. Other questions emerged with the triumph of Sufi leaders over traditional forms of authority in West African society in the early twentieth century. For example, what was the spiritual identity and social role of women in the new religious order of the Sufi shaykhs? To these questions, Shaykh Ibrāhīm devoted separate sections of the *Kāshif.* The book has immediate

Aḥmad Dem. For specifics of this debate and reference to these rare manuscripts, see Seesemann's forthcoming book "Divine Flood," chap. 3, "Seeing God." I am indebted to Seesemann for providing me with an advance copy of this and other chapters.

[10] *Kāshif,* 266.

relevance to some of the more contentious issues that continue to confront Muslims of our own age: the orthodoxy of Sufism and its practices, the untenability of continued racial and cultural prejudices, the nature of religious authority, and the ethics of disagreement between Muslims.

Conventions of writing change with the times, and Sufi literature is no exception. That roughly half of the *Kāshif* consists of citations from prior works should not surprise one familiar with the development of the genre of Islamic scholarly prose since the eighteenth century. The source analyses conducted on important Sufi works in the region immediately prior to the *Kāshif*—on Ibn Mubārak al-Lamaṭī's *Ibrīz* (written in 1719 in Morocco) and 'Umar al-Fūtī Tal's *Rimāḥ* (written in 1844 in Senegal) by Bernd Radtke,[11] and on Malik Sy's *Ifḥām al-Munkir al-Jānī* (written in 1921 in Senegal) by Ravane Mbaye[12]—permit a useful comparison to Shaykh Ibrāhīm's citations from previous sources. According to Radtke, the *Ibrīz* contains 270 citations from 139 different books, with most sources used not more than once or twice. The *Rimāḥ* contains about 640 citations from 123 sources, with most citations (two-thirds) coming from nine authors (with eighteen to ninety-eight citations from each). Mbaye did not keep track of the number of citations in the *Ifḥām,* but he estimates more than two hundred sources,[13] while six works are cited more frequently (between four and thirty citations from each). In the *Kāshif,* Shaykh Ibrāhīm used 271 citations from 112 different works. There are eighteen works which Shaykh Ibrāhīm cited more frequently: from between four and seventeen times each.

A closer look at the main sources used in each of the three seminal Tijānī works—the *Rimāḥ,* the *Ifḥām,* and the *Kāshif*—reveal a diverse source base for Tijānī writers in West Africa. Of the main sources listed by Radtke for al-Ḥājj 'Umar, Mbaye for al-Ḥājj Mālik, and ourselves for

[11] Bernd Radtke, "*Ibrīziana:* Themes and Sources of a Seminal Sufi Work," *Sudanic Africa* 7 (1996); and Bernd Radtke, "Studies on the Sources of the *Kitāb Rimāḥ Ḥizb al-Raḥīm* of al-Ḥājj 'Umar," *Sudanic Africa* 6 (1995).

[12] Ravane Mbaye, *Le grand savant El Hadji Mālick Sy: Pensée et Action,* vol. 3, Ifham al-Munkir al-Jani: *Réduction au silence du dénégateur* (Beirut: Dar Albouraq, 2003).

[13] This number may be inflated, as an examination of Mbaye's "Index of Works Cited" for the *Ifḥām* reveals that Mbaye neglects to distinguish between works cited by Sy directly and works referenced by authors whom Sy cites. For example, Shaykh Ibrāhīm Niasse may cite from al-Sha'rānī, who in turn cites from a work of Ibn al-'Arabī. In such a case, our list of the sources in the *Kāshif* would not include the work of Ibn al-'Arabī, only the work of al-Sha'rānī.

Shaykh Ibrāhīm, the only work cited more than four times by all three writers was the primary text of the Tijāniyya: ʻAlī Ḥarāzim al-Barāda's *Jawāhir al-Maʻānī.* Shaykh Ibrāhīm shared al-Ḥājj ʻUmar's frequent recourse to the works of ʻAbd al-Wahhāb al-Shaʻrānī (d. 1565, Egypt), Aḥmad Zarrūq (d. 1493, Libya), and Ibn ʻAṭā-Allāh (d. 1309, Alexandria), and to Ibn Mubārak al-Lamaṭī's *Ibrīz.* Shaykh Ibrāhīm also shared al-Ḥājj Mālik's predilection for the nineteenth-century Moroccan Tijānī scholar Ibn al-Sā'iḥ's *Bughyat al-Mustafīd* and the eighteenth-century Turkish Sufi exegete Ismāʻīl al-Haqqī's *Rūḥ al-Bayān.* To this list of distinguished Sufi writers, Shaykh Ibrāhīm added frequent use (four or more citations each) of the writings of the Malian Qādirī Shaykh Mukhtār Kuntī (d. 1811), Ibn al-ʻArabī al-Ḥātimī, Abū Ḥamīd al-Ghazālī (d. 1111, Baghdad), the Moroccan Shādhilī scholar Ibn ʻAjība (d. 1809), the Moroccan Tijānī Shaykh Aḥmad Sukayrij (d. 1949), the Persian Sufi al-Qusharyī (d. 1072), the Indian scholar Aḥmad al-Ṣāwī (d. 1825), the Mauritanian Shādhilī master Muhammad al-Yadālī (d. 1753), and the writings of al-Ḥājj ʻUmar himself.

Space limitations preclude a comprehensive list of the sources as included in the analyses of Radtke for the *Ibrīz* and the *Rimāḥ.*[14] But an overview of the sources for the *Kāshif* sustains Radtke's observation for these other works concerning the diversity of subject matters drawn from. Like al-Lamaṭī and al-Ḥājj ʻUmar, Shaykh Ibrāhīm cited works of exegesis (*tafsīr*),[15] Prophetic traditions (Hadith),[16] jurisprudence (*fiqh*),[17]

---

[14] I have included a list of the works cited three times or more in the appendix of the forthcoming translation of the *Kāshif.* See Wright, Holland, and El-Okene, *Removal of Confusion.*

[15] Most notably the *Tafsīr al-Jalālayn* of Jalāl al-Dīn al-Suyūṭī and Jalāl al-Dīn al-Maḥallī (along with the marginal commentary of Aḥmad al-Ṣāwī), the *Jawāhir al-Ḥisān* of ʻAbd al-Raḥmān al-Thaʻālibī (d. 1471), the *Rūḥ al-Bayān* of Ismāʻil al-Ḥaqqī, the *Tafsīr al-Kabīr* of Fakhr al-Dīn al-Rāzī (d. 1210), the *Baḥr al-ʻUlūm* of Abū Layth al-Samarqandī, and the *Taʼwīlāt al-Najmiyya* of ʻAlā' al-Dawla al-Simnānī (d. 1336, Persia).

[16] Aside from the six *Sunan* of al-Bukhārī, Muslim, Abū Dāwūd, al-Tirmidhī, Ibn Māja, and al-Nasā'ī, these include the following: the *Musnad* of Aḥmad b. Ḥanbal, the *Muwaṭṭa'* of Imam Mālik, the *Shifā* of Qāḍī ʻIyāḍ, the *Kitāb al-Adhkār* of al-Nawawī, the *Sunan al-Kubrā* of al-Bayhaqī, the *Al-Maqāṣid al-Ḥasana* of al-Sakhāwī (d. 1497, Egypt), the *Fatḥ al-Bārī* of Ibn Ḥajar al-ʻAsqalānī (d. 1448, Egypt), the *al-Fatāwā al-Ḥadīthiyya* of Ibn Ḥajar al-Haythamī al-Makkī (d. 1565, Mecca), and other classical works of Prophetic traditions.

[17] These are predictably mostly of the Mālikī school (*madhhab*), such as the *Risāla* of al-Qayrawānī (d. 996, Fez), the *Mukhtaṣar* of Khalīl, or the *Bidāyat al-Mujtahid* of Ibn Rushd. But there are a few notable exceptions, such as the Shāfi'ī scholar ʻAbd al-Mālik

theology (*'aqīda*),[18] grammar (*naḥw*),[19] religious principles (*uṣūl*),[20] and history/biography,[21] as well as works of Sufism. The geographical diversity of sources also deserves notice: authors from India, Persia, Turkey, the Arab Middle East and Morocco are cited alongside authors from West Africa.

The diversity of subjects and geography demonstrate definitively that West African Muslim writers participated in global Muslim currents of scholarly exchange. The *Kāshif* was certainly no exception in this regard. Indeed, Shaykh Ibrāhīm would have had to rely almost exclusively on the library of his father, al-Ḥājj 'Abd-Allāh Niasse (d. 1922), to write the *Kāshif.* Although the Shaykh, who attained scholarly fame at a young age, would have undoubtedly begun his own collection of books by the early 1930s, he did not travel outside of Senegal until 1937, many years after writing the *Kāshif.* A comparison of the sources for the *Kāshif* with those used by al-Ḥājj Mālik Sy for the *Ifḥām al-Munkir al-Jānī* reveals the same basic corpus of rich and varied Arabic literature for West African scholars of the early twentieth century.

Outside of the predictable recourse to past Tijānī writers, a few authors deserve special note for their frequent citation by Shaykh Ibrāhīm: 'Abd al-Wahhāb al-Sha'rānī (d. 1565, Egypt), Muḥammad al-Yadālī (d. 1753, Mauritania), and Mukhtār al-Kuntī (d. 1811, Mali). After classic Tijānī works such as the *Jawāhir al-Ma'ānī,* Shaykh Ibrāhīm quoted from various writings of al-Sha'rānī more than any other author. He described al-Sha'rānī in his author's appendix to the *Kāshif* as "the saintly pole and scholarly gnostic, he who combines the Sacred Law with the

---

Abū al-Ma'ālī al-Juwaynī (known as Imām al-Ḥaramayn, d. 1085, Hijaz) and Imām Badr al-Dīn al-Zarkashī al-Shāfi'ī (d. 1392).

[18] Such works include important works of the 'Asharī school--for example, the *Sharḥ al-Mawāqif* of 'Alī b. Muḥammad al-Jurjānī (d. 1413), the *Idā'at al-Dujannat* of al-Maqqarī (d. 1632, Tlemcen/Damascus), and the *al-Durr al-Thamīn wa al-Mawrid al-Ma'īn* of al-Mayyāra (d. 1662, Fez).

[19] Among the works cited in this category are the *Al-Qāmūs al-Muḥīt* by Abū al-Ṭāhir b. Ibrāhīm Majd al-Dīn al-Fayrūz Ābādī (d. 1414, Shiraz/Mecca) and its commentary *Tāj al-'Arūs min Jawāhir al-Qāmūs* by al-Zabīdī (d. 1790, India/Egypt).

[20] An example would be the *Al-Asrār al-'Aqliyya* by the Egyptian Shāfi'ī scholar Taqiyy al-Dīn al-Muqtaraḥ (d. 1215).

[21] Such works would include the comprehensive history of the early Muslim community by al-Ṭabarānī or the historical compilation of legal opinions in the Maghrib, the *Mi'yār* of al-Wānsharīsī.

Divine Reality."[22] The *Kāshif* contains seven citations from al-Sha'rānī's *Laṭā'if al-Minan wa al-Akhlāq,* two citations from his *Kitāb al-Jawāhir wa al-Durar,* two citations from the *Baḥr al-Mawrūd fī al-Mawāthiq wa al-'Uhūd,* two citations from the *Mīzān al-Kubrā,* one citation from *Al-Ṭabaqāt al-Kubrā,* one citation from the *Al-Yawāqīt wa al-Jawāhir,* and three citations from al-Sha'rānī where the work is not mentioned. This gives a total of eighteen citations from al-Sha'rānī.

The significance of al-Sha'rānī for Shaykh Ibrāhīm's popularization of Tijānī Sufism in West Africa should not be overlooked. Al-Sha'rānī has been variously described as the one who spread and interpreted the teachings of Ibn al-'Arabī for a larger Muslim audience[23] or as the half-eloquent, half-vulgar Sufi realist whose writings played an unmistakable role in popularizing complex Sufi doctrines.[24] There is no doubt that al-Sha'rānī's eloquent popularization of Sufism paralleled Shaykh Ibrāhīm's own historical mission to open the teaching of *ma'rifa* to a larger audience. Consider this striking statement from al-Sha'rānī cited in the *Kāshif* concerning the essential accessibility of complex Sufi doctrines: "A special characteristic of the Sufi spiritual path is that if a genuine seeker enters this path, he becomes familiar with the technical terminology in every detail, from the first step he takes on this path. It is almost as if he himself is the creator of this terminology."[25] Elsewhere al-Sha'rānī was quoted as speaking to the commonsense application of Sufi practice attainable by every practicing Muslim:

> Know that the science of Sufism is knowledge kindled in the hearts of the saints, until the practical application of the Qur'ān and the Sunnah completely illuminated their hearts. For anyone who puts the religion into practice like this has such sciences kindled in him, along with moral virtues, secrets and Divine realities which tongues are incapable of enunciating.[26]

This justification of Sufism resonated with Shaykh Ibrāhīm's attempt to inspire ordinary Muslims with Sufi understandings, particularly with

---

[22] *Kāshif,* 244.

[23] Chodkiewicz, "Diffusion of Ibn 'Arabi's Doctrine."

[24] Michael Winter, *Society and Religion in Early Ottoman Egypt: Studies in the Writings of 'Abd al-Wahhab al-Sharani* (New Jersey: Transaction Books, 1982), p. 233.

[25] Citation from al-Sha'rānī (unidentified source), as quoted in *Kāshif,* 249.

[26] *Kāshif,* 105.

ma'rifa, the "direct knowledge of God." When discussing the "legal status" (*ḥukm*) of Sufism in the first chapter of the *Kāshif,* Shaykh Ibrāhīm cited the adage of al-Shādhilī: "If someone does not become immersed in this science of ours, he will die as one who persists in the major sins, without being aware of his condition."[27] In a revealing poem written years before the drafting of the *Kāshif,* Shaykh Ibrāhīm said explicitly: "Whoever does not obtain knowledge of the Merciful, his life has been in ruin for all time spent."[28] The work Sha'rānī did in popularizing and rationalizing Sufi doctrines (from the perspective of Muslim Sunni orthodoxy) was clearly indispensable for the sense of urgency with which Shaykh Ibrāhīm wished to inspire his fellow Muslims to obtain the experiential knowledge of the Real through the science of Sufism.

Shaykh Ibrāhīm's use of two great West African Sufis of the eighteenth century, al-Yadālī (of the Shādhilī order) and al-Kuntī (of the Qādirī order), is also of interest. He was of course not the first to have recognized the scholarly aptitude of these writers, but the extent of his reliance on them seems unprecedented. The *Kāshif* contains five substantial citations from al-Yadālī, mostly from his writings on Sufism such as the *Sharḥ Khatimat al-Taṣawwuf.* This is a bit more than the number of times this author is cited by al-Ḥājj Mālik in the *Ifḥam,* one of the few other books of the genre where al-Yadālī's name appears. The writings of Kuntī, mostly his *Al-Kawkab al-Waqqād fī faḍl dhikr al-mashā'ikh wa ḥaqā'iq,* is cited in the *Kāshif* thirteen times. This far surpasses the four times he is cited by al-Ḥājj 'Umar in the *Rimāḥ.*[29] Brita Frede, a research fellow at the Zentrum Moderner Orient in Berlin studying the Mauritanian disciple of Shaykh Ibrāhīm, "Shaykhānī" Menna Abba, has made an interesting observation that Shaykh Ibrāhīm's use of al-Yadālī and Kuntī would have been particularly effective in the scholarly milieu of the Idaw 'Alī in Mauritania, the Tijānī stronghold where Shaykh Ibrāhīm was gaining an influence at the time of the *Kāshif*'s writing.[30]

This specific historical context aside, the citations from al-Yadālī and

---

[27] *Kāshif,* 42.

[28] Shaykh al-Islam Ibrāhīm 'Abd-Allāh Niasse, "Rūḥ al-adab" [Spirit of good morals]. See Shaykh Hassan Cisse (translation and commentary), *The Spirit of Good Morals by Shaykh of Islam Ibrahim Niasse* (Detroit: African American Islamic Institute, 2001), p. 70.

[29] Radtke, "Sources of the *Kitāb Rimāḥ,*" 100–101.

[30] Welcome observation made by Frede at my presentation of the *Kāshif,* "Reflections on the *Kāshif al-ilbās* of Shaykh Ibrāhīm Niasse," for the Tijānī literature conference, "The Tijani literature of Africa," sponsored by ISITA, Fez, Morocco, June 2009.

Kuntī play an important role in advancing Shaykh Ibrāhīm's argument in the *Kāshif.* The force of the citations from al-Yadālī included in the *Kāshif,* which speak openly of key Sufi concepts like annihilation and absorption in God a century before Sufi orders became widespread in West Africa, might suggest that al-Yadālī's role in the popularization of Sufism in West Africa may have been underestimated. In any case, the inclusion of an earlier well-respected Mauritanian scholar speaking openly of "gnosis" (*ma'rifa*) through "annihilation" (*fanā'*) was significant for Shaykh Ibrāhīm's public emphasis of the necessity of *ma'rifa.* Kuntī's role in the development of Sufism in West Africa has been well substantiated,[31] so it is not surprising to find his name among the sources for the *Kāshif.* It is nonetheless of note to find the specific use Shaykh Ibrāhīm found for this scholar so closely linked to the emergence of Sufi orders in West Africa. The *Kāshif* generally presents Kuntī as an earlier example of a consummate spiritual trainer, guiding aspirants to the knowledge of God through the process of *tarbiya.* As earlier mentioned, *tarbiya,* or "spiritual training," was the key practice through which the "flood" of gnosis was to reach Shaykh Ibrāhīm's followers. It is no accident then that Shaykh Ibrāhīm cited Kuntī at length on the subject of master-disciple relations within Sufism, asserting the guide's authority to train followers and the respect which the aspirants are supposed to accord their teacher. Significantly, it was the presence of the guide, rather than the guide's words, which was emphasized here: "The shaykh is he who polishes you with his virtuous character traits, trains you by bowing his head in silence, and enlightens your inner being with his radiance."[32] The idea of a teacher who would enlighten his student through his inner radiance was certainly a key concept in the transmission of *ma'rifa:* especially since *ma'rifa* is incapable of being fully enunciated.

The *Kāshif* thus presents an adept weaving together of the writings of past Sufi masters. This format was of course not lost on Shaykh Ibrāhīm himself, who described his own work as one that "collects the cream of the books authored on this discipline (of Sufism)." It was a style well received by his contemporaries. In the section of commendation of the *Kāshif,* Shaykh Ibrāhīm included the praise poetry of a number of scholars

---

[31] See Aziz Batran, *The Qadiryya Brotherhood in West Africa and the Western Sahara: The Life and Times of Shaykh al-Mukhtar al-Kunti, 1729–1811* (Rabat: Université Mohammed V, 2001).

[32] Mukhtār al-Kuntī, as cited in *Kāshif,* 144.

from Mauritania associated with the heritage of Muhammad al-Ḥāfiẓ al-Shinqīṭī (d. 1830), who first introduced the Tijāniyya south of the Sahara. The Shaykh wrote:

> I have presented my work entitled *Kāshif al-Ilbās* to a community among the people of my age, the influential notables (*ahl al-ḥall wa al-'aqd*),[33] people of scholarly criticism in the sciences of the Sacred Law and the Divine Reality. They are the masters of creation and leaders of the distinguished folk of the Sufi Path. All of them, praise be to Allah, praised me for this work and wrote a commendation. So I wanted to include here their commendations and testimonies in order that the fair-minded person would know that this book contains nothing other than a collection (*jam'*), so the words in it are the words of the scholars (*'ulamā'*), and the doctrine on which it is built is the doctrine of the bosom-friends.[34]

This ability to gather the knowledge of the prior scholars was thus considered an important testimony to a shaykh's scholarly credentials. Certainly the work played a role in the submission of many within the Idaw 'Alī scholarly tribe to Shaykh Ibrāhīm beginning in the 1930s. This may also have been the case in Nigeria. According to Shaykh Tijānī 'Alī Cisse, when Shaykh Ibrāhīm first visited Nigeria in 1945, he took with him four copies of the *Kāshif,* which he left with the *'ulamā'* in the city of Kano, one of the most renowned centers of Muslim scholarship in Africa. After reading the book, the Kano scholars testified that such a work gathering so much knowledge together in one place was an occurrence they thought relegated to the scholars of Islam's golden ages.[35]

---

[33] The *ahl al-ḥall wa al-'aqd* is an idiomatic expression in Arabic, translated literally as "the people who bind and unbind." The expression connotes a sense of authority. I am indebted to Muhammad Sani Umar and Rüdiger Seesemann for their suggestions here.

[34] *Kāshif,* 289.

[35] Shaikh Tijānī 'Alī Cisse, in discussion with the author, Medina-Kaolack, Senegal, June 2009. Rüdiger Seesemann reports a similar version of events from Barham Diop, the traveling companion of Shaykh Ibrāhīm: "On his departure from Kano, Shaykh Ibrāhīm left behind a few copies of *Kāshif al-Ilbās.* Later the book found its way into the hands of a few religious scholars, who assumed that the author had lived in Senegal a long time ago—until 'Alī Cissé and Abu Bakr Serigne Mbaye (Niasse) made a stopover in Kano on their way to the Hijaz. The scholars of Kano were stunned by their visitors: 'Where are you from?'—'Senegal.' Then the scholars asked whether they had heard about a saint called Ibrāhīm Niasse, who had lived in Senegal a long time ago. 'He is alive, he is still in Senegal. This is his brother.'"

This is not to say that the *Kāshif* contains nothing original. In his analysis of the sources for al-Ḥājj 'Umar's *Rimāḥ,* Radtke rightly draws the reader's attention away from the fact that the author incorporates so many other sources, focusing instead on *how* the author uses his sources. The *Kāshif* of course also does contain a good deal of the author's own prose and poetry. But the methodology the Shaykh used in citing from other works deserves a closer look. Generally speaking, Shaykh Ibrāhīm presented a series of citations on a given subject that were usually interspersed with his own comments. He usually concluded by including what Shaykh Aḥmad al-Tijānī (d. 1815), the founder of the Tijāniyya Sufi order, had himself said concerning the subject in question. The significance of this straightforward approach should not go unnoticed. In fact, Shaykh Ibrāhīm says in the text: "Whoever examines it (the *Kāshif*) closely and judges it fairly will know for certain that this compilation was authored by Shaykh al-Tijānī with his own hand." The guiding spiritual presence of Shaykh Aḥmad al-Tijānī aside, Shaykh Ibrāhīm's methodology in selecting and ordering citations seems to have been consciously aimed at demonstrating the dialectic between the Tijāniyya and prior Sufi traditions, thereby giving fresh perspective to Shaykh al-Tijānī's own words. Moreover, Shaykh Ibrāhīm hoped that such fresh perspective would benefit and unite his Tijānī readership, praying in the book's conclusion that Allah would "make it a source of discernment for the Spiritual Path and its people, stringing them together (like pearls) in the company of the Noble Seal (al-Tijānī)."

The claim that Shaykh al-Tijānī was the real author of the *Kāshif* of course has broader implications than just putting the Shaykh Tijānī's words in dialogue with other Sufi traditions. In fact, the *Kāshif,* like many other Sufi texts, has developed its own reputation for saintly blessing (*baraka*) simply as a physical object. Shaykh Ibrāhīm writes: "May Allah put tremendous blessing (*baraka*) in it, to the extent that it may bless any place it is found." Today, many followers of Shaykh Ibrāhīm carry the book with them when they travel just to have the blessing of it in their possession wherever they go.[36]

Standards of Muslim sainthood and saintly blessing—where personal agency is often obscured with reference to God, the Prophet Muḥammad, or a previous saint—should not prevent the reader from grasping the

[36] Shaikh Tijānī 'Alī Cisse, in discussion with the author, Medina-Kaolack, Senegal, June 2009.

unprecedented or original quality of Shaykh Ibrahim's *Kāshif al-Ilbās*. The *Kāshif* argues in a nutshell that acquiring the experiential knowledge of God (*ma'rifa*) is the essential purpose of human existence, and that a "flood" has come within the ranks of the Tijāniyya to spread the Sufi path of Seal of Saints, Shaykh Aḥmad al-Tijānī, thereby reconnecting people to the Divine in a time of ignorance and distance from God. Even if the *Kāshif* is filled largely with a collection of the "cream" of past Sufi writings, Shaykh Ibrāhīm's essential argument was extraordinarily bold and unprecedented. That he was aware of this is substantiated by his frequent warnings in the text not to reject the pronouncements of God's saints. The result of this weaving together of the Sufi tradition to justify the concept of a flood of gnosis was no less than the foundation for one of the most successful Sufi revivals in modern times. The significance of the *Kāshif* in the development of modern West African Muslim religious identity cannot be underestimated.

Whatever the blessing or lofty purpose of a Sufi text, the reader of the *Kāshif* should not forget the suspicion with which Sufis have generally treated writing. "Secrets are in the hearts of the distinguished folk (*rijāl*), not in the bellies of books," Shaykh Ibrāhīm Niasse was fond of saying.[37] Indeed, very particular circumstances inspire a Sufi master such as Shaykh Ibrāhīm to write in the first place, and most Sufi shaykhs left no writing at all. The purpose of Sufi texts is to respond to particular issues at hand, not to serve as the means of actually transmitting the knowledge of God or the means of purifying the ego-self (*nafs*). These essential aims of Sufism are meant to be transmitted from spiritual master to disciple in the absence of texts. The *Kāshif* was written to make space for the emergence of the Tijānī flood, not to actually initiate aspirants into the knowledge of God brought by this flood. Sufi texts remain important sources for study not because they contain the actual practices of people, but because they help establish a conceptual space within which practice unfolds.

[37] Shaikh Hassan Cisse, in discussion with the author, Lagos, Nigeria, February 2006.

Pezeril, Charlotte. ***Islam, Mysticisme et Marginalité: Les Baay Faal du Sénégal.*** Paris: L'Harmattan, 2008. 320 pp.; ill., glossary, bibliography. €31,50 (paper).

This academic monograph is the first to focus exclusively on the Baye Fall as a distinct movement, rather than merely a heterodox offshoot of the more "mainstream" Mouridiyya Sufi order. Although a detailed ethnography of modern Baye Fall communities is at the heart of the study, Charlotte Pezeril's narrative is far from static. Its four parts encompass a long and highly self-reflexive statement on the author's field experience and methodology, a social and intellectual history of the movement, numerous biographical sketches of individual followers, and an ethnography-based "thick description" of current Baye Fall social and religious life. The great strength of the book is the wealth of oral source material upon which it draws. The author gained access to a large number of Baye Fall murid from different age-groups and social backgrounds in both urban and rural communities, and this insider's perspective is reflected in the rich and detailed descriptions of key beliefs and practices as well as in the emphasis on diversity within the movement.

The study is conceptually framed as a reflection on marginality. Key questions are how and why the Baye Fall became socially and religiously marginalized and how one can account for the expansion and continued popularity of the order in spite of this marginality. Pezeril addresses these questions by examining how the dynamic interaction of insider and outsider perspectives has informed how the Baye Fall has evolved over time. The central argument in her account of the early history of the Mouridiyya is that the emergence of the Baye Fall as a distinct order was a gradual process and that, in spite of reformist tendencies within the Mouridiyya, the relationship between Mourides and Baye Fall remains symbiotic. In what Pezeril calls the "Baye Fall imaginaire" (i.e., the set of key narratives and values that emerge from the oral sources), Ibrahim Fall is considered the "father" (Wolof: *baye*) of the movement only in the sense that his followers seek to emulate Ibra Fall's absolute devotion to his Sheikh,

Islamic Africa, VOL. 1, NO. 1, 2010. ISSN 2154-0993. www.islamicafricajournal.org

Ahmadou Bamba, the founder and spiritual center of the Mouridiyya. The author emphasizes that the question of what differentiates the Baye Fall from the Mouridiyya is perceived as incongruous by Baye Fall who see their "father" Ibrahim Fall as the "lamp" that rendered Ahmadu Bamba's sainthood visible, just as the Prophet Muhammad is the "Bab Allah" (Door to God).

After the deaths of Bamba and Fall, spiritual authority within the Mouridiyya came to be shared by different lineages, and those murids attached to the marabouts of Ibrahim Fall's family increasingly emphasized the emulation of Fall, both in his servitude to Ahmadu Bamba, now embodied by Bamba's lineage, and in his distinct physical appearance—unkempt hair, patchwork attire, and large leather belt. The visibility of the Baye Fall increased with their expansion into the cities from the 1940s, leading to the further reinforcement of group identity. This process coincided with the emergence of urban elite that had been educated in colonial schools and had internalized a colonial modernization narrative that was highly critical of the "backward" and "exploitative" marabout-murid relationship at the heart of Sufi practice. From the perspective of colonial and Senegalese elites the distinct attire and way of life of the Baye Fall came to epitomize everything deviant and outdated about the Sufi orders.

Pezeril identifies two distinct ways in which the Baye Fall has responded to critiques both from within the Mouridiyya and from outsiders. She shows that, like Sufis elsewhere, the Baye Fall has responded to reformist discourses with the redrawing of group boundaries and increased emphasis on educating followers in the basic teachings and principles of the *tariqa.* The second response has been the embrace of marginality as a mode of self-valorization and sign of Divine election. This response is particularly central to modern Baye Fall trajectories, which are described in the fascinating final part of the book on globalization, fragmentation, and conflict. Pezeril compellingly argues how urban poverty, mass migration, and cultural globalization have led to great transformation and differentiation in what it means to be Baye Fall. Although many Baye Fall are still focused on labor in service of the marabout and spiritual education in the *daara* (Wolof: Qur'anic schools), some of the impoverished urban youth have come to associate the external features of the movement with cultural nationalism, political protest, and even Rastafarianism. Conflict over the meaning of "Baye Fall-ness," and particularly what some perceive as the urban "criminalization" of the order, is aptly expressed in the modern distinction made by the "guardians" of the tradition between Baye Fall and Baye "Faux."

Pezeril's study convincingly recasts the often misunderstood and exoticized history and teachings of the Baye Fall as an integral part of the wider Mouridiyya movement. Ibra Fall's distinctive "path" of hard physical labor, total submission to his Sheikh, and even his failure to fast and pray appear less idiosyncratic in light of the wider Baye Fall "imaginary" drawn out by Pezeril. Oral sources show that, rather than mere self-mortification in blind submission to a marabout, the spiritual *objectives* of Ibra Fall's unusual bodily discipline did not differ significantly from those of either the Mouridiyya or other Sufi orders. The disciplining of the ego, detachment from the physical world, and, ultimately, achieving nearness to God are as central to Baye Fall teachings as they are to the wider tradition of Sufism. By drawing parallels between the Baye Fall "path" and the wider Sufi tradition of Islam, Pezeril shares the concerns of other recent studies of Sufism in Africa that seek to move beyond the study of "African" Islam as a purely local phenomenon and demonstrate how local Sufi movements are inserted in the global flow of Muslim ideas and practices. It is somewhat unfortunate, however, that the author's presentation of the Baye Fall as the "moderate" and "universalist" alternative to Muslim "fundamentalism" (304), combined with an explicit desire to vindicate Baye Fall practice as "authentically Sufi" (150), causes her to reaffirm the notion of an essential contradiction between a supposedly open and tolerant mysticism on the one hand and a rigid, necessarily conservative and potentially aggressive legalism on the other a dichotomy that has its origin in normative Protestant notions about the primacy of personal faith over ritual practice and that continues to be a dominant trope in popular as well as academic work on Sufi practice. Her assertion that Muslim mysticism "peut être envisagé comme une mode d'être à Allah qui veut dépasser la praxis coranique pour en découvrir l'essence cachée" (128) may be an accurate description of some articulations of the Baye Fall path (which, as Pezeris has shown us, are not monolithic) but cannot be generalized to Sufi thought in general, which more often than not poses scrupulous adherence to the Shari`a as a crucial prerequisite for spiritual progress.

Rahma Bavelaar, Northwestern University

Jonathan Miran. *Red Sea Citizens: Cosmopolitan Society and Cultural Change in Massawa.* Bloomington: Indiana University Press, 2009. 394 pp.; glossary, bibliography, index, 5 maps, and 35 black-and-white photographs. $27.95.

It has never been easy for specialists to situate Northeast Africa in broad terms or the *longue durée.* Astride the academic fault line between Africa and Middle East area studies, the field has for some time been partitioned by contemporary national politics, sectarianism, and orientalist legacies, leaving many scholars ambivalent towards synthetic or long-term analysis.[1] In recent years, however, a number of historians have developed new approaches to the field: some have turned away from the study of states and ethnicities to engage questions raised by urban or colonial historians elsewhere in Africa and Asia, while others have reconceptualized the definition and boundaries of the region itself, as with the recent interest in Sudanic and Nile Valley history. To these projects we can now add Jonathan Miran's provocative new book, a wide-ranging study of how developments in the Red Sea arena fostered social, economic, and political change in nineteenth- and early twentieth-century Massawa, a predominantly Muslim port city in present-day Eritrea. It is a nuanced and refreshing look at the links between the local and the global in Northeast Africa.

After an introduction outlining the author's main themes and sources, the first two chapters of the book situate the Eritrean coast within a range of regional and interregional systems. Chapter 1 explores the history of Massawa before the nineteenth century, focusing first on the emergence of local power brokers in the early Ottoman period and then on the decline of their political autonomy in the nineteenth century as Ottoman indirect rule yielded to open competition among Egyptians, Italians, and Ethiopians. Chapter 2 sets these developments against the backdrop of a larger Braudelian conjuncture in the Red Sea arena: Miran argues here that commercial and imperial developments in the nineteenth century transformed Massawa from an entrepôt to a shipping emporium that linked the

[1] Notable exceptions include Donald Crummey, *Land and Society in the Christian Kingdom of Ethiopia: From the Thirteenth to the Twentieth Century* (Chicago: University of Illinois Press, 2000); Jay Spaulding, *The Heroic Age in Sinnar* (East Lansing: Michigan State University, 1985); James McCann, *People of the Plow: An Agricultural History of Ethiopia, 1800–1990* (Madison: University of Wisconsin, 1995); and Teshale Tibebu, *The Making of Modern Ethiopia, 1896–1974* (Lawrenceville, N.J.: Red Sea Press, 1995).

Mediterranean and the Indian Ocean to the regional economy. The next three chapters explore the impact of these trends on the port and its environs. Chapter 3 illustrates how the growing Hadrami and Egyptian presence in Massawa led to the emergence of a new group of merchants who made their fortunes by mediating between the coast and hinterland. Chapter 4 explores how Islamic culture bound these communities together and defined Massawa as an urban space, and chapter 5 examines a cohort of urban notables who exemplify these various developments. In many respects, these final chapters represent the crux of the author's arguments—it is here that we see how life in cosmopolitan Massawa often turned upon "the aspiration to create unity in a context of social diversity" (6). A conclusion summarizes the arguments and briefly surveys twentieth-century developments.

There is much here that will fascinate the specialist. Miran's wide-ranging discussion of the Islamic institutions and networks of the coast represents a major contribution to the literature, particularly since he links them to revival movements in the wider Muslim world. The analysis of the growth of the local Khatmiyya and 'Ad Shaykh groups is especially rich, and the discussion of their relationship with the Italian authorities is fascinating—it would seem that the Muslims of colonial Massawa occasionally resembled their counterparts in the Sudan or northern Nigeria in that they could obtain limited forms of autonomy that were denied to other groups. Most of the oral testimonies, local Arabic histories, and *qâḍî* court records that inform this discussion are previously untapped sources. Equally penetrating is the author's rich analysis of the regional economy: his detailed discussion of pearl diving documents the range of local and extra-local actors (African divers, Arabian captains, Hadrami and Indian financiers, and European consumers) to great effect, as does his comparison of Massawans' involvement in the regional caravan routes and slave trade, though he readily admits the tentative nature of his findings on the last subject on account of the available sources.

Yet as much as Miran deepens our understanding of these ostensibly local topics, his major contribution lies in the links he draws with much larger historical processes. On the one hand, he has introduced a framework for thinking about the integration of Northeast Africa into the larger Indian Ocean arena in the modern period, and the analysis is greatly enriched by recent scholarship in that field. For example, his discussion of brokerage systems and port-hinterland relations is driven by comparisons with the East African coast, and his account of the Hadrami diasporic presence in Massawa is informed by the growing literature on that topic. Yet on the other hand, Miran's work is also notable in the extent to which it links Northeast Africa to developments in the Middle East. Ottomanists have recently turned to the study of imperial peripheries, and the present work draws upon, and contributes to, this literature, particularly in chapter 1. At the same time, Miran's work casts a new perspective on Egyptian imperialism in the region, which has heretofore been understood in terms of its conquest of the Sudan.

Miran's work admirably illustrates how attention to transregional empires and larger spatial units can recast the problems that animate a field. Though some might be challenged by the author's open rejection of the conventional, state-based periodization of Northeast Africa, others will find this a stimulating intervention that poses a host of new questions. Chief among these is the possibility of extending Miran's model of conjunctural and sociocultural change—is this new kind of cosmopolitan culture exceptional, or is it in fact more widespread in the region? Equally significant is the question of the fate of cosmopolitans in the ensuing era of nationalism, a fascinating subject to which the author alludes in the conclusion. Miran has set a high standard for those who wish to take up these topics.

James De Lorenzi, CUNY, John Jay College

Aḥmad b. al-Mubārak al-Lamaṭī. ***Pure Gold from the Words of Sayyidī 'Abd al-'Azīz al-Dabbāgh (Al-Dhahab al-Ibrīz min Kalām Sayyidī 'Abd al-'Azīz al-Dabbāgh).*** Translated and annotated by John O'Kane and Bernd Radtke. Leiden and Boston: Brill, 2007. 1,016 pp. $250. (cloth).

This enormous volume represents a type that is rarely considered worthy of translation. It is a collection of the words of 'Abd al-'Azīz al-Dabbāgh, the Moroccan Sufi shaykh of the late seventeenth to early eighteenth century (died 1132/1719–20), as recorded by Aḥmad b. al-Mubārak al-Lamaṭī, a scholar who was also a disciple. Besides the general bias toward earlier works in the study of Sufism, most texts selected for translation are theoretical expositions, poetry, or hagiography, or at least belong to a definable genre. This work, however, is part hagiography, part idiosyncratic esotericism, and a good deal more. For those interested in understanding later Sufism, about which there are significant gaps in our understanding, it is a treasure trove of information. Many of the ideas elaborated here are not found in classical texts, but they remain relevant today. (The Sufi shaykh who was my chief informant in my research on Sufism in modern Egypt recommended it, and we studied it together in Arabic.) The translators state that they have not been able to find any evident sources for al-Dabbāgh's Muhammadology and his views on the prophetic nature of certain dreams, which they regard as unique. Of course, even in the case of Ibn al-ʻArabī we cannot know whether his writings reflect his original ideas or ideas that were current in his time; this is even more the case with a text from a later period concerning which there has been much less research. Suffice it to say that some of the ideas encountered here—for example, the necessity of having a waking vision of the Prophet in order to attain illumination, the inheritance by a disciple of the "secrets" of his shaykh when he dies and other aspects of the shaykh-disciple relationship, and the impact of illumination on the individual Sufi's mind and body—are all vital aspects of popular Sufism today. Bernd Radtke's earlier writings pointed out the misunderstandings that abounded concerning the notion of "Neo-Sufism"; the translators believe that this work clarifies many of the erroneous statements that have been made on that topic.

This translation is indeed a two-man work: Radtke translated the text from Arabic into German, and John O'Kane translated it from German into English. The translation is remarkably clear and readable. The one feature of their translation that is unconventional—and, to this reader, occasionally discordant—is the ubiquitous use of contractions, even in sentences that deal with dense theoretical issues (e.g., "a dreamer who's received illumination" [11], or "without sight one can't see" [18]). The translators are aware that few people are likely to read the book through in its entirety and that some portions will prove challenging to the modern reader. They have provided a detailed and useful outline of the entire book in the first 112 pages, with page numbers frequently noted, enabling the reader to go directly to specific areas of interest. A summary outline may also be found at the beginning of each chapter. Some of the anecdotes that appear in al-Dabbāgh's biography and in the section on the shaykh-disciple relationship are quite entertaining; these and other portions could be used even in undergraduate courses on Sufism.

This translation will undoubtedly expand scholarly awareness of this little-read but influential book, which reflects a still understudied period in the development of Sufi thought and practice.

Valerie J. Hoffman, University of Illinois at Urbana-Champaign